Baseball Graffiti

by

Edwin Howsam

8 April 2003

Martin —
You're a great ski instructor. I
hope you enjoy my little baseball book.
Good luck with your ski video,
Cheers!

To my father and mother,

Bob and Janet

We few, we happy few, we band of brothers.

— William Shakespeare

Henry IV

Baseball scouts are often underpaid, overworked, and unappreciated by those in the hierarchy of baseball. And yet there isn't a group of professionals anywhere in this country who love their work more than baseball scouts. Their love for the game is unflinching.

Contents

Introduction

I was disillusioned when I returned from Vietnam in December 1968. I grieved for my friends who had returned in body bags. It was a confusing period that I still haven't completely sorted out.

I spent the next year at Camp Pendleton, California. By the time I was discharged from the Marine Corps, my wife, Nancy, and I had saved some money — she had been an elementary school teacher in Denver living with her parents while I was receiving combat pay in Vietnam as well as my officer's salary — so we decided to do something different.

But a small matter detained us in Denver — the birth of our first child, Erik. Six months later, after renting a U-Haul, we drove to Quebec City, Canada.

If we had had the money we might have gone to Europe, and if we hadn't had a child we might have ended up in Mexico, but Québec was a splendid compromise. It was a foreign country within a foreign country.

Nancy and I took French language courses, we met people from all over the world, I wrote some short stories, and I started to scout for the Cincinnati Reds in the spring.

These were happy times. I was alive, young, and in love. Erik was a constant joy, so full of life.

I can remember walking through the quaint streets of Quebec City, watching the great Guy Lafleur play hockey as an amateur, skiing at Mont Ste-Anne, buying wonderful berries in the open-air marketplace, playing softball with Mormon missionaries, closely following the debate on Québec separatism, eating popcorn and watching Hockey Night in Canada, and singing Erik to sleep every night in a rocking chair.

But I can also remember experiencing cabin fever in our basement apartment, watching people water their lawns in the spring to melt the snow and ice, suffering through a cold spell when it reached twenty below zero every day for six weeks, and watching a car race on ice at the Winter Carnival with a wind chill factor of one hundred below zero with my friend, Gérard Laplante.

After a year it was time to move on. I had received a job offer from my father, the general manager of the Cincinnati Reds, to live in Arizona and to scout in the Southwest. Images of a sunbaked desert, swaying palm trees, and swimming pools made the decision easy.

What I found when I joined the Cincinnati Reds scouting staff was a group of men who were extremely talented, friendly, hard-working, and absolutely loved what they were doing. It was very refreshing.

We did get to Arizona in August 1971. There *was* a sunbaked desert, swaying palm trees, and swimming pools. I did scout for the Cincinnati Reds for 17 years. This book is a reflection of those years.

— Edwin Howsam

Scottsdale, Arizona

December 1994

Acknowledgements

While writing this book I was helped by numerous people, but especially by Erik Howsam and Cathy Ballman. Their intelligent comments have greatly shaped this book. Their loving fingerprints are everywhere. I offer them my heartfelt thanks.

There are many people to thank in baseball, but the two people I *must* thank are Les Houser and Don Gust. Both were part-time scouts who worked for me. Both of their families treated me like a son. I've spent many wonderful hours with the Housers and the Gusts. Their kindness and friendship won't ever be forgotten.

I also would like to thank the research department at the Baseball Hall of Fame Library. I have called innumerable times to verify names, places, dates, and statistics. They always answered my questions.

Roy "Hardrock" Johnson
(EDWIN HOWSAM)

1

Hardrock

I've always enjoyed being around older people because they have experienced so much of life. I love to listen to their stories. I like to hear about the dreams they pursued. I want to know about their lives — the laughter and the tears.

It was, therefore, only natural that Hardrock Johnson and I became friends after I moved to Arizona and started scouting there. He had been around the baseball block. There was so much I could learn from him.

When I think of Hardrock now, definite images appear . . . . .

• I can see him sitting in a lawn chair at Scottsdale Community College's field. A lazy foul ball that the catcher can't quite reach, barely clears the backstop and hits Hardrock squarely on top of the head. Fortunately, he's wearing a hat as he almost always does, but he doesn't flinch or say a word.

• I can remember hearing him talk about Jackie Robinson's baseball skills in glowing terms. This isn't an easy thing for a man to do who grew up in Oklahoma, in a different age, and with a different set of values.

• After watching a game in Tucson and driving back to Phoenix on Interstate 10, a white Ford speeds by me going 80 mph. All I can see of Hardrock is his hat.

• I'm sitting with Hardrock at a high school playoff game. Two players' dads are sitting behind us. They start to get on the home plate umpire. Hardrock, who has a short fuse, turns around and says, "What the hell do you know about umpiring?" The two men, getting a kick out of some old man getting so riled up about nothing, start to chuckle. I have to restrain Hardrock from going after them with his cane.

*   *   *

Let's roll back the years to a spring day when the sun was brighter, the grass greener, and the crack of the bat louder.

Roy "Hardrock" Johnson is watching a high school baseball game. He's sitting in a lawn chair, one foot up against the screen, his cane hooked to the screen, stopwatch in hand, and hat pulled low across his brow. Hardrock scouts Arizona for the Chicago Cubs and watches anything from high school games to big league spring training games.

For almost 60 years he has been a big league pitcher and coach, minor league manager, and scout. His life in baseball spans from Ty Cobb to Johnny Bench, and from Connie Mack to Sparky Anderson.

"I always liked Ty Cobb," Hardrock said, without taking his eyes off the hitter. "I liked anyone who played with that much intensity and who put that much effort into baseball. I had an awful lot of respect for him. So did the fans. But they didn't like him in Philadelphia. He had had lots of trouble there in the early days. He would do anything to beat you — show you up, spike you, fight, anything.

"I hadn't been with the club too long, and one day in Philadelphia the pitchers were throwing at Cobb. We had a bunch of guys who were good bench jockeys, and they were hollering things at Cobb, and I was laughing on the bench. The pitcher knocked him down. The next pitch Cobb tried to drag one and drug it foul. He tried to make the pitcher cover first base, so he could cut him up.

"After seeing that I started hollering. Connie Mack, who liked me, said, 'Hey, Johnny, come over and sit down beside me. A couple more of those guys holler at him and he's going to be right in this bench on top of them. I don't want him jumping on you.' Cobb was a rough customer."

Hardrock clicked his stopwatch as the hitter legged out a hit.

"Connie Mack never wore a uniform when he managed, and he never missed or forgot anything. He was a gentleman and one of the nicest men I've ever known, but by God I've heard him tie into people — they had it coming of course — and he was the most vicious man I ever heard. Worse than John McGraw or anybody else. He could think of more things to say to you, and he always had you right.

"But the players liked him awful well. If you were having a bad day, he wouldn't jump up and down and scream at you like some of the college and high school coaches do yelling at the kids on the field. He wouldn't treat a kid like that."

Hardrock shook his head when he mentioned Babe Ruth. "You

couldn't have believed it unless you would have been there. This was near the end of Ruth's career. I was coaching with the Chicago Cubs, and the wind was blowing hard and steady in from right field, coming off that lake with no letup. We were talking about it before the game, how Ruth won't bother us any today. The rest of the ballplayers hit balls hard into right field, which would have been out of the ballpark the day before, but that day the outfielders had to come in to catch the fly balls.

"It was Ruth's third time up, and we had them beat 8 or 9 to 1. He hit the first pitch, barely foul, plum out of the ballpark. We were sitting there talking about it — goddamn, how did he hit a ball so hard into that wind?

"The very next pitch — across the street there are some apartments and as long as I was there watching left-hand hitters I never saw anyone hit that building — he hit the next pitch fair and up so high on the building that we didn't even have to get up from the dugout. Ruth didn't move. He didn't move until after the ball was out of the park. He turned around and said something to Gabby Hartnett and then trotted around the bases. I saw Gabby drop his head so no one would see him laugh. We had such a good lead that you could actually appreciate it.

"So when the inning was over I went by Gabby and asked him what the Bambino had said. Gabby said Ruth had said, 'Let's see the wind stop that one.' That was the hardest hit ball I ever saw."

Hardrock glanced over my way after a called third strike.

"Back in 1935, my first year as a Cubs coach, we were going along pretty good — won 19 straight games in Chicago — but we had to go into St. Louis and win two out of three to clinch the pennant.

"We got to St. Louis that morning by train. We went to our hotel and went in for breakfast. There was quite a write-up in the newspaper — not on the sports page — but on the front page about how Dizzy Dean said they were going to beat us.

"A little later on we went out to the ballpark and Charlie Grimm, the manager, called a team meeting. About that time the clubhouse door flies open and in walks Dizzy Dean talking. No one knew what was going on. Diz says, 'Oh, Charlie, you're having a meeting. I didn't know you was having a meeting.' He walks over to Charlie — Charlie had a score card in his hand — and he pulls the score card out of his hand and says, 'Let's get this meeting over and bring in the band and have some music.' Diz had a little old band with him — three or four guys who played during the game — waiting outside the clubhouse.

"We thought Charlie would throw him out of there, but Charlie never said a word. Diz kept on talking and says, 'Let's go over these hitters right fast. Who's going to pitch?' Of course, he knew who was going to pitch.

Warneke had a score card in his hand and he had been advertised to pitch. So Diz commenced calling off the hitters and telling Warneke how to pitch to each one, and actually he was telling him exactly what Grimm or Hartnett would have told him.

"For instance, when Diz got to Medwick, the big outfielder, he says, 'Pitch this guy low and away. Don't give him anything high or he'll beat you with that pitch.' Diz was talking just so serious. He told us how to pitch to guys we had never seen — guys they had just brought up like Johnny Mize. Diz got down to Leo Durocher and says, 'Just don't walk him.' When he got to his brother, Paul, he says, 'Don't worry about him either, he can't hit. But that guy who's pitching tomorrow, you better bear down on him.'

"Diz got through with all the hitters, and Charlie Grimm says, 'That's okay with me. Bring on your hillbilly band.' Diz brought in the band and they played for us.

"We had players who were real superstitious and they hadn't changed sweat socks since we got in that winning streak and they hated awful bad to put on those road uniforms cause we had used home uniforms for the 19 straight wins. They hadn't laughed and guys like Jurges were all serious, and by God the players began to laugh. Diz had loosened up our club.

"That first game went to the seventh inning nothing to nothing. Paul Dean pitched good against us. He was a high-ball pitcher. Phil Cavarretta hit a home run over the right field fence and we won the ball game 1-0.

"Hell, I thought Paul Dean throwed a lot harder than Diz. But he wasn't near the pitcher. He didn't have the curveball Diz had, and Diz pitched down. Diz was a real good pitcher.

"Anyway, Diz pitched against us in the second game, and Big Bill Lee, the curveballer, pitched against him. We beat them, I believe it was 4 to 2, and we cuffed Diz around pretty good that day. Lee pitched a good ball game and clinched the pennant for us. We lost the third game and our winning streak stopped at 21 games."

Hardrock managed in Bisbee from 1927 to 1932 in the Arizona State League. Both he and his wife have fond memories. Mrs. Johnson recalled, "The darnedest thing, this little mining town, you wouldn't think you could get imported French dresses for our daughter but you could. I'll always remember those handmade French dresses. They were made by nuns in Paris and how they got to Bisbee I don't know."

Hardrock said, "There was lots of interest in baseball out here then. They drew awfully good in some places. You could pretty near count the population of Bisbee at the ball game. I remember once when we were playing over at El Paso. They always had a good club and we were rivals. We drew seven thousand people. Many of them were on the field. The big leagues opened that day in the East and the St. Louis Browns had six thousand people."

Traveling was over poor roads in the heat and dust. "I remember one of those trips we made," Hardrock said. "Of course, I was the bat boy, bus driver, and manager. We had an old bus and it was the worst thing you ever saw. It was always breaking down, or having a flat tire, and I had an awful time stopping it.

"One time we left after a ball game on a Sunday and I was going up a long grade. I started to shift to a lower gear but couldn't get it in there and I couldn't stop the damn thing and it started back down the hill just flying. I was 30 minutes picking up my ballplayers. They were opening up those doors, jumping out the doors, jumping into cactus beds and everything else."

A relief pitcher was warming up when Johnson explained how he got the name Hardrock.

"We were playing down in Tucson," he said, "and I got run out of the ball game. They put me out of the ball park and there stood a big gray horse with a saddle on it someone had tied to a hitching post. So I got on this old gray horse and rode him up to the fence just to where I could see real good. I sat there on him and no one paid any attention to me, so I managed the game from on top of that horse.

"Finally, a few innings later the umpire spotted me and got me off the horse. The next day Pop McKale — he did a little sportswriting in the summer in those days — had quite a write-up. About how our club had beat the Tucson club, and about the good prospects on our team, and how the boys had hustled and battled when their manager had been throwed out. He also said that they had to hustle for that old hardrock manager. The kids began to call me Hardrock and when I went to the big leagues as a coach everyone called me Hardrock."

Not only was the Bisbee manager a character, he also had a few playing for him. "I had this one kid who had been in the Navy. He had come down to us from the Hollywood ball club where he was drinking a lot and wouldn't show up to the ballpark. He was a third baseman and could have been a big league ballplayer. He was a good hitter and had good power.

"This day we were facing a hard-throwing sidearm pitcher, who later pitched in the big leagues. We got some men on and needed a base hit, so I called him out to hit. He wasn't playing because he had a bad leg. I was coaching third and I met him and told him this guy is throwing hard and be ready up there. He looked at me — he was half asleep anyhow — and said, 'He throws it over the plate, don't he?'

"He walked up there — you know that big background there in centerfield in Tucson — and hit the first pitch not a foot from the top of it with the damnedest line drive you ever saw. It whistled out there. Pretty near knocked that board over. You could hear that ringing all over Arizona."

Because Miami, Arizona, is down in a canyon, maybe it wasn't heard there, but a lot else was heard in the wild playoff of 1929. "That playoff in Miami was never finished," Hardrock said.

"We were playing the seventh game over there and it was getting dark. The ball game was tied going into the ninth — it was a big score. Both clubs had run out of pitchers and so in the ninth inning the first man up for us hit a home run, the next a double, another run was hit in, and as the second run crossed home the crowd started out on the field, wanting the umpire to call the game on account of darkness. But it wasn't so dark that my hitters couldn't see and hit the ball.

"I charged out to where the umpire was to protect him. Before I got there this big cowboy hit me in the face with his cowboy hat. He got back out of the way and this other cowboy ran up, but some of my ballplayers got in my way and the cowboy said, 'Let him go. I'll take care of him.' I hit him all the way from here to there. The umpire was beginning to wilt by that time. They had him scared to death. At that point I wouldn't have cared if they would have got him.

"There was a big battle and I followed the umpire to the clubhouse. They weren't going to let him in so I kicked down the door. I was trying to get the umpire to start the game again. He said, 'No, no. We can't go out there. It's getting too dark. You wouldn't want me to go out there and get killed, would you?' I told him that he didn't have a gut in his body.

"It was quite an ending. There were all kinds of arguments. They did call the ball game. I hadn't thought of not finishing the series but our directors with us said don't play them, you won the series. We packed up and went home to Bisbee and never played it.

"There was more publicity about it in the Eastern papers. Some writer in the East got a hold of it. It didn't hurt baseball with all the interest it generated, I'll tell you that. The writer was impressed by how seriously the fans took the game. Guess he never knew how much money those miners and cowboys had bet on it. I got the biggest kick out of it after it was all over."

As Hardrock watched a player score from second base, he said, "Might be wrong about it, but it seems like I never saw a real good ballplayer back in those days loaf down to first base even if he hit the ball back to the pitcher. They didn't save themselves like they do now. Of course, there's better equipment today and the ball is much more lively now. We played for one run then. It's difficult to compare the players because the game was different in those days. There were more guys who could bunt and drag bunt then. All these guys now think that you're trying to show them up if you ask them to bunt. We had better hit-and-run men then than they do now. Every club had two or three guys who could hit behind the runner."

Hardrock always arrives early to scout a game. "There's a lot you can learn before a game ever starts. And you don't always get to see everything you want to see during a game. For instance, I've gone to see a good-looking hitting prospect, and the other team has intentionally walked him every time up, or I've gone to see a highly-rated shortstop and I never get to see him make the long throw from the hole. See what I'm saying. So I watch batting practice to see how a player hits and what type of power he has. I watch infield practice so I can evaluate a player's arm, hands, and range. I watch everything. Players who stand around don't impress me. Then I watch the game to see what he can do under game conditions. Of course, you're looking for players who have tools, natural abilities, especially those who can run and throw. That speed plays a very important part in baseball.

"In pitchers I look for the pitcher who has a good delivery, who has an aptitude for pitching, who has good size, who has good control — isn't afraid to throw strikes — and most of all, who has a good arm. A guy who can throw hard. A pitcher can learn those fancy pitches later, but no one can give a pitcher a good arm just as no one can give a player speed. Those are things that he is born with.

"I don't like pitchers who labor out on the mound, or those who are herky-jerky. And another thing I like to see is a pitcher who is a little mean out there. My pitching philosophy has always been to let the hitters smell that horsehide. Don't let any hitter dig in on you and get those good cuts. Knock 'em down!"

For years Hardrock and his big brown French poodle, Jacques, scouted baseball games together. Jacques was a fixture at Phoenix Municipal Stadium. Many contended that Jacques was the best baseball scout in the area because he always napped when there wasn't a prospect playing, and was always alert when one was playing. He smelled out the good ballplayers. Jacques had to be put to sleep last year and Hardrock sure misses him.

A few years ago Hardrock was watching a game at Phoenix College with Jacques at his side. He was sitting in his lawn chair when suddenly it collapsed. People nearby gasped. From the ground Hardrock looked up at Jacques and asked, "Well, Jacques, was I out or safe?"

*   *   *

I'm sitting with Hardrock at a spring training game. The crowd rises for the national anthem. Hardrock struggles to stand up but he can't. I try to help him but he's too proud and won't let me. I know how much this is hurting him inside because he is so patriotic, but more than that, we both know what this means.

Hardrock Johnson and I were friends for 15 years before he died in 1986 at the age of 90. He was every inch a man, a man with true grit, and because baseball was his passion and his life's work, the consummate baseball scout.

NOTABLE QUOTES

When Thornton Lee struck out Babe
Ruth on a knuckle-curveball, the Babe
yelled out at him,
"Hey, kid, is that your masterpiece?"

— Spring training game
Birmingham, Alabama

"You may not believe it at your age, Ed,
but the great thing about baseball is that
it keeps you around young people."

— Rosy Ryan
pitched for John McGraw's New York Giants;
General Manager, Phoenix Giants

Four-seam Fastball
Bill Jackson — Major League Scouting Bureau
(EDWIN HOWSAM)

2

A Tournament

Scouts like tournaments. Tournaments let the scout see many players at one location, thus cutting down on time and travel.

But not all tournaments were productive. I used to attend junior college tournaments in February in places like Yuma and Tucson at the spring training sites of the San Diego Padres and the Cleveland Indians. The teams would play their games at a complex of four fields. This made it easy to scout the games. I could turn in any direction, walk a few feet, and watch another game.

But these early games were deceptive. It always seemed like the good players never played well, and all the sandblowers (little guys) would hit the ball out of the yard. Pitchers, who had looked great six months before, couldn't find the plate, gave up lots of hits, and looked awful. It could be confusing, but the experienced scout had been through it all before. True talent would emerge later on.

The late summer tournaments were excellent. By this time a lot of baseball had been played. Genuine phenoms would materialize under the crucible of a tournament.

*   *   *

Connie Mack World Series, August 11-18, 1989

This is the Silver Anniversary of the Connie Mack World Series in Farmington, New Mexico. I've been scouting the tournament since 1971, and I've only missed one year, 1981, when the Reds scouts were taken off the road in August because of the baseball strike.

The span of 17 years is a large slice out of anyone's life, and to return year after year to the same place means more than just scouting a tournament.

It means meeting tournament officials, fans, reporters, radio announcers, coaches, players, umpires, bat boys, local business people, judges, oil engineers, priests, square dance callers, and others. It means developing friendships, knowing people who fall in love, marry, bear children, divorce, re-marry, get promoted, get fired, get rich, get poor, move away, stay put, and die.

I was dead tired when I drove into Farmington that first August in 1971. Joe Bowen, the Reds Scouting Director, was breaking in the rookie scout right. He wanted me to scout different tournaments with different scouts across the country, learning as much as possible from some of the best scouting minds in the business.

I had started my tour of tournaments at Johnstown, Pennsylvania, scouting it with Joe Bowen, Elmer Gray, and Joe Caputo. Then I drove to Wichita to scout the national semi-pro tournament with Fred Uhlman, a man with a delightful sense of humor. But Fred could destroy you. He was always as fresh as a flower. Games would start at eight in the morning and continue long past midnight. We would go back to the hotel and have a few drinks, and maybe get two or three hours of sleep. After a week of this, I couldn't have told you if Babe Ruth, Ty Cobb, or Walter Johnson were playing in the tournament. I would have said Ruth had no power, Cobb wasn't aggressive enough, and Johnson's fastball was short.

After Johnstown, Wichita and Farmington, I ended this tour of tournaments in Tucson, scouting the American Legion World Series with Larry Barton, Jr. We were close in age and struck up an instant friendship. Bill Almon was the top prospect in the tournament. Almon had written to all the clubs in the spring telling them not to waste a draft on him because he was going to Brown University. San Diego had drafted him anyway in the tenth round. Three years later in 1974, San Diego would again select Almon in the draft, only this time as the first pick in the country.

Anyway — to retrace my tread marks — I had met Larry Barton, Sr. (Larry Jr.'s father) that first time in Farmington. He was an older gentleman with a bad hip, a constant chew of tobacco in his mouth, and a sparkle in his eye. He had spent his whole life in baseball as a player, manager, and scout. Larry exuded pure joy at a ballpark. When we would discuss ballplayers, he would always ask me, "Well, Ed, what can he do? What can he do?"

Farmington was special from the beginning. The people were friendly; the tournament was well-run, well-supported, and had quality players; and hot dogs cost 15 cents. The location — Tony Hillerman country — was hypnotic: the majestic Rockies an hour to the north, ancient Anasazi ruins in every direction, the surrounding southwestern landscape with its dramatic buttes and mesas painted in rich, earthy colors, and — not least to an avid trout fisherman — one of America's great trout rivers, the San Juan, flowed nearby.

The tournament's place on the calendar is important as well. The scout's year starts off in January in a slow walk and thunders into a mad dash to the June draft. The summer work, although less stressful, involves more travel while running tryout camps, scouting professional teams and amateur tournaments. By August you're exhausted from all the travel, from the heat, from all the games seen. Then suddenly you're back in Farmington where the horizon stretches forever under a turquoise sky, where the cool evenings invigorate, where you can relax and unwind, where the baseball is good, and where the wearing of cowboy boots is *de rigueur*.

The relationship between scouts is relaxed as well. The competition to find players in the spring for the June draft is over. No one is in a pressure cooker at Farmington. An ambiance of friendliness exists. Some scouts bring their golf clubs to play in the golf tournament, some scouts bring their fishing poles to try their luck on the San Juan, and some scouts bring their families.

Many a morning in the dawn's pink I've found myself in chest waders in the ice-cold San Juan playing a rainbow or brown trout on a wet fly or Panther Martin lure, knowing that I had an afternoon game and two evening games to scout, and thinking that it just doesn't get any better than this in baseball scouting.

Hospitality in Farmington is legendary. The entire community backs the tournament. The teams are greeted at the airport by the Connie Mack Queen and Princesses and Kelly Greens; there is a dance, a barbecue dinner, a golf tournament, a hospitality room, a parade, a baseball clinic, and a Foster Parents Program where fans provide room, board, and transportation for two players while their team remains in the series.

The Connie Mack World Series is for boys from ages 16 to 18. The standard of play and the quality of players is first-rate. Since I've been scouting the tournament, well over twenty former players have reached the major leagues. In 1987, Ken Griffey, Jr., a center fielder who played for the Cincinnati Midland Redskins team, was the first player selected in the June draft. The next year, Mark Lewis, a shortstop who played on the same Cincinnati team, was the second player chosen in the draft.

Who scouts the Connie Mack World Series? On a quick tally I count scouts from twenty-four clubs and a representative from the Major League Scouting Bureau, plus coaches from colleges such as Wichita State, Arizona, Texas A&M, and Southern Cal.

In my opinion this year's crop of prospects is very good. There are eight players in the tournament who are interesting: four who are legitimate prospects, four who are marginal.

The four players I consider to be legitimate prospects are Frank Rodriguez, shortstop, New York team; Shane Andrews, catcher, Farmington, New Mexico team; Calvin Murray, center fielder, Dallas, Texas team; and Todd Van Poppel, right-handed pitcher, Dallas, Texas team.

Frank Rodriguez has the best arm in the tournament for a position player. I haven't seen him run all out, so I'm not sure how well he runs. He has shown a little power at times. He's decent in the field — his hands and range are good enough. Frank also pitches and shows an average major league fastball (90 mph). At this stage in his development, I'm not sure if he'll end up being a shortstop or a pitcher. He has two ways, therefore, to get to the big leagues. But sometimes this can become a curse if the college coach abuses the situation. I have seen players ruin their arms (and careers) because they were playing a position in the field when they were called in to pitch, and hadn't sufficiently warmed up their arms. Anyway, my report will say that Rodriguez has some ability, and his progress should be followed very closely next spring. It's my guess that he'll be drafted somewhere in the middle rounds next June.

I have seen Shane Andrews play for the last two years. He isn't having a good tournament (fine with me, let the other scouts change their minds on him), striking out almost every time at bat because he's trying to hit every pitch out of the park. No problem. This youngster is tough, coachable, has power (hit the longest home run I've ever seen hit in the tournament last year), has arm strength (throws in the low 90s off the mound), and has a linebacker's physique. He hasn't caught much, so his catching skills are crude, but with experience and good instruction, his skills will be good enough someday. I project that Andrews will be drafted in the top three rounds next June.

Calvin Murray *was* Cleveland's first round pick in June. He's an exciting, make-something-happen type ballplayer. He can play center field right now in the big leagues. In last year's tournament, he played third base and I liked him there as well. His arm is good enough from either position. This guy can run (4.06 seconds to first base). He's struggling a bit at the plate this year, but that doesn't bother me. What you have here is an excellent athlete. The rumor floating around the tournament is that Murray turned down an outstanding offer from Cleveland: at least 200 G's, plus the college scholarship plan. Supposedly the boy and dad wanted to sign, but the mom wanted him to go to the University of Texas. I guess you know who calls the shots in that family.

Todd Van Poppel pops his fastball good enough for me. He's the best kid in the tournament. In fact, I project him to be a high first round pick next June. He has the classical pitcher's physique: tall and slender (6-5, 185), sloping shoulders, long arms, big hands, a good, loose arm with movement on his fastball, and a free and easy delivery. Actually, his delivery is so deceptively easy that I can't believe he's throwing as hard as he is — up to 94 mph. Moreover, his breaking pitch is impressive for a young pitcher. I can't help but like this boy.

It was after midnight when Harry Pritikin, a part-time scout with Kansas City, and I pulled into a parking space at the Holiday Inn. We had been to the hospitality room. We were surprised to see Joe Hayden, the coach of the Cincinnati Midland Redskins team, walking in the parking lot and puffing on a cigar.

Hayden is an interesting guy. He's a successful businessman in Cincinnati; he always wears shorts on the field; he's a former roommate and great friend of Bo Schembechler (many of his good players end up at Michigan); and he has the players' interests at heart.

We asked him what he was doing walking in the parking lot at this time of night. He said he was thinking about his pitching staff, which had not performed well in the tournament. We talked about his pitchers, past players, Bo, Pete Rose, gambling, whether players should sign out of high school or go on to college, and the player he's most proud of on this year's team, Mike Hill, a black outfielder raised in the projects and Harvard-bound after the tournament.

Hayden's teams are always well-coached and talented. He runs a tight ship. He's coached some excellent players, including Bill Doran, Barry Larkin, and Ken Griffey, Jr.

Hayden symbolizes what is best about Connie Mack baseball. He's a fiery competitor on the field, but when the game is over, he keeps everything in perspective.

When I think about Farmington over the years, various images appear as if I were watching a slide show.

Click. I'm watching the parade with Edith Kennedy and Mrs. Foutz downtown in front of Russell Foutz Indian Room where I've bought some wonderful Navajo rugs. Mrs. Kennedy, who has a granddaughter in the parade, is telling us how she and her husband two years ago took care of two players from Latham, New York, as foster parents. They still keep in touch and the boys sent her flowers when her husband passed away.

Click. Angie McLamore is singing the National Anthem before one of the games. This petite gal belts out a fine rendition. She's as cute as a button, as bubbly as shook-up Pepsi, and a gifted student. I know her parents. Mac is the local high school baseball coach — maybe the best in New Mexico — and her mom is an elementary school principal.

Click. Here comes Hayden Boyce holding his mom's hand. Linda points out to the field where Danny Boyce, the coach of the Farmington team, is standing. Hayden shrieks, "Daddy! Daddy!" Danny acknowledges him with a slight smile, playing it cool. But I've known the family for a long time. No father ever loved his son more than Danny loves his little man.

Click. I'm sitting with the other scouts in a long row of chairs behind the backstop. Some scouts are pointing their radar guns at the pitcher; others are jotting down grades and comments in their scouting books.

Click. I talk to Father Gerard at the game. It depresses me greatly to know that soon Father Gerard will not be able to watch baseball, since he's going blind. He tells me that he has prayed for the Cincinnati Reds that day. He tells me that every time I see him. He's originally from Cincinnati.

Click. There's good ole boy Jack Weatherford. He has an Okie accent, a heart of gold, a love for bawdy jokes, a deeper love for baseball, a voice that can be heard from three fairways over, and the charm to sell you flood insurance in the middle of the Sahara — yes, siree, folks — bring your shovel when you're around Jack.

Click. I'm fishing the San Juan with different fishing buddies: Lee Boyce (Danny's dad), who tells absolutely the worst jokes in the world; Red Means, the best fisherman I ever fished with; Bill Smith, an Okie who would literally give you the shirt off his back; Griz Johnson, a scout who simply loves to fish; and Clark Crist, another scout who fell in love with the San Juan.

Click. The umpire John Kelly comes over to the screen and says hello. He's working behind the plate today. Kelly has come up from Phoenix to work the tournament. I usually see him and his partner, John Toppi, working high school and junior college games around the Phoenix area. I've known them both for years. I always stop to talk to them in the parking lot before the game while they're putting on their gear. They're always friendly. We never discuss umpiring.

Click. I stop by to see Louie and Helen Fayad. They own a mom-and-pop restaurant just up the road from Farmington. We always have an argument about whether I'm going to pay for the meal. Our families go back a long way. They are about the hardest working people I know. The hard work has paid off; they have put their three children through college and all three were honor students. The American dream is alive and well in Aztec, New Mexico.

Click. Jim Thomas, a sports writer for the *Farmington Daily Times*, and I are stacking up empty beer cans on a table in the hospitality room when another reporter does a headfirst slide onto the table à la Pete Rose, knocking the cans from here to breakfast.

Click. I'm talking with Linda Onuska about her two kids in the hospitality room just before closing time as her husband, Paul, a prominent judge in town, wipes off the tables.

The Connie Mack World Series at Farmington, New Mexico, is *special*. It blends the surrounding physical beauty with the spiritual beauty of a community pulling together to produce a wholesome show of young men, strutting across the baseball stage, doing their very best.

*   *   *

How good were my evaluations on the four players that I liked in the 1989 tournament? As a follow-up, let's compare my draft predictions to what actually happened.

Frank Rodriguez really must have come on in the spring, since he was taken by the Boston Red Sox in the second round of the June 1990 draft. He didn't sign but went to Howard Junior College in Texas. Boston, who still retained the rights to him, signed Rodriguez right before the June 1991 draft for $400,000.

Shane Andrews also went higher in the draft than I thought he would go. He was taken by the Montreal Expos in the first round of the June 1990 draft and signed for $175,000.

Calvin Murray went to the University of Texas. He was taken as the seventh pick in the first round of the June 1992 draft by the San Francisco Giants. He signed for $825,000.

Todd Van Poppel — the best player in the June 1990 draft — wasn't selected until the fourteenth pick of the first round by the Oakland A's because he had told all the teams that he was going to the University of Texas. Oakland gambled that big money would change his mind. It did. He became the first high school player to receive a million-dollar-package deal in the draft. Van Poppel signed for 1.2 million dollars: $500,000 as a signing bonus, and $700,000 for a three-year major league contract. (Bo Jackson was probably the first drafted player to receive a million-dollar-plus package deal, but nobody knows for sure.)

I also made some "big bucks" from the June 1990 draft. I won two dinners from a rookie scout who said Van Poppel wouldn't go in the first round, and Andrews wouldn't go in the top three rounds.

Jim Pettibone
(EDWIN HOWSAM COLLECTION)

3

Bone

Over and over I've heard many scouts say that the way they discovered a good ballplayer was purely serendipitous. They had gone to see a certain player and an unknown player had outshined the player they had gone to see. This is how I stumbled on Jim Pettibone.

In March 1980 I was at Coronado High School in Scottsdale, Arizona, along with many other scouts, to watch the top prospect in the state pitch his first game. The top prospect didn't have a good game, but the other team's pitcher had a very good game. He threw a nearly average major league fastball (87-89 mph), threw a wicked curveball at times, and showed a competitive fire that can't be taught.

I saw Jim pitch in four other games that spring. I was becoming highly interested in this 17-year-old kid. He threw 90 mph at times, he had the makings of a *great* curveball — I didn't see a better curveball from the big leaguers in spring training that year — and he had the size to go with it. In addition, he was a good kid from a good family *and* he did eat and sleep baseball.

There was interest in Pettibone, but not as much as I thought there would be, especially after his impressive outing against Coronado. However, two excellent scouts stayed hot on the trail and both were serious threats — Gene Thompson, a scout with San Francisco, and Bill Jackson, a scout with the the Major League Scouting Bureau.

A fortuitous thing happened in late spring during the high school playoffs. Pettibone had pitched too much during the regular season and his arm was tired. The "heavies" — scouting directors, cross-checkers, and supervisors — were there to see him pitch. These men were to be feared because if a player had a good game in front of them, then the odds of getting that player in the draft dropped significantly. Pettibone did not have a good game. He hardly threw any fastballs and his curveball was mediocre. I went home elated.

I had Larry Barton, Jr. come over from California so that we could work Jim out before the draft. Barton, a former minor league catcher with an exceptionally good track record with pitchers, caught Pettibone. Barton liked what he saw. Things were really looking up now.

On June 3, 1980 the Cincinnati Reds selected James Fred Pettibone, right-handed pitcher, Saguaro High School, Scottsdale, Arizona, in the second round of the baseball draft. He signed four days later.

*   *   *

"I started playing baseball with the East Scottsdale Little League when I was 7 years old. I pitched from the beginning. I loved to pitch. It was just the best to be the guy out there on the mound. The main guy. If you did well, you won, and if you did bad, you lost. I played other positions but it was real fun to try to throw the ball by somebody.

"My dad never pushed me but I know he wanted it as much as I did. He knew I had some talent even when I was young. He had been a good athlete and a good catcher, so he started catching me in the back yard. He caught me up until the day he really got down with cancer. Remember that little makeshift screen and the mound and rubber that I made in the back yard? Before we put that screen up, dad would catch me off that mound. There were times when I realized that he was getting a little bit too old because the ball would hit off the glove, but he would stick right in there. He would tell me to go ahead and let it go. When he got cancer real bad, he ended up getting behind the screen and just putting his glove up for me and sitting on a five-gallon bucket. And then I'd throw into the screen and he would just move the glove around for me and tell me what I was doing right or wrong.

"I always knew that he was backing me. He was a serious guy in a great way. If I wouldn't hit the glove or if I wasn't concentrating or if I made the same mistake twice, he would roll the ball back to me — halfway. I would have to walk up and get the ball and then walk back to the mound. And he wouldn't say a word. What he was trying to do was get me to gather myself and realize what I was doing wrong.

"Did you see the movie *Field of Dreams*? Me too. Remember that scene where the father and son are playing catch? It brought tears to my eyes.

"I didn't pitch one inning as a freshman. I played right field but I hardly played at all. They had a football coach who was the baseball coach and he ended up playing his favorites, who were football players. Anyway, I went from my freshman year to the Phoenix Winter Baseball Instructional League and got together with Joe DiCaro and Joe Carbarcio. It was great because you would pick a position that you wanted to play, and then they would give you a lot of individual instruction.

"The following year I played sophomore baseball, which would be junior varsity. I pitched minimal and played a little out in the field. I went to Phoenix Winter Baseball again and got a lot of help and started developing my pitching skills. They had an all-star game and I pitched in that. That is the first time I can remember scouts being around. Obviously, they weren't looking at me, who was I? I threw 83 mph, which was the hardest anyone threw. All of sudden there were some eyes opened.

"My junior year I wound up getting cut from the varsity team. That shattered me. Blew me away. For a junior to get cut it's all over with. But the coach asked me and a couple of other juniors who had also been cut if we wanted to play another year of JV ball, and I thought, why not? So I went down there and pitched and had a great time. I was with four other juniors and the rest were sophomores, and one time we played the varsity in an intersquad game and just beat the crap out of them. The varsity had a lousy season and I was called up near the end of the season.

"Phoenix Winter Baseball started up again and there were scouts in the stands. My name was going around. Arizona State started asking questions about me. I was excited.

"Before the season started my senior year, we had a two-week period where the players worked out but the coaches couldn't be there. I had gotten that thing rolling. Later the guys voted me a captain and I ended up being the starting pitcher.

"There must have been fifteen scouts in the stands when I threw against Coronado. Kendall Carter was All-World and was 11-1 with a 0.68 ERA his junior year, and I got to throw against him. My heart was just shooting. I can't explain the amount of adrenalin that shoots through you when these guys are up there pointing their guns at you. You want to throw the ball through the mitt, through the screen, and through that damn gun that they have pointing at you. It's the biggest rush that you could ever imagine.

"Anyway, they beat us 7-4 and I gave up a home run and I walked a few guys and got a few strikeouts, and I went home that night and I was really down. I thought that I had screwed things up. Later that night Bill Jackson called me and asked me if I liked baseball, if I saw a future career in baseball and things like that. He was feeling me out. He asked me what I thought of my performance, and I told him I was kind of down. He said, 'Hey, Jim, you have a lot of people looking at you.' After talking to him, I was fired up again. The next game there were some scouts in the stands to see me pitch.

"It went around school and I got a lot of recognition for it. It was a bonus because I had gotten cut the year before. The scouts just kept watching me all spring long. I was getting a lot of letters from colleges I had never heard of, asking me if I wanted to come there and offering partial scholarships, full scholarships. It was great. Boy, if I could relive those days!

"One thing I did — and I probably shouldn't have done — was throw a 7-inning game and the next day I would be in the outfield throwing as hard as I could. I never had an arm problem, never had a twinge, never could feel that my arm was tired. Lots of times I didn't give my arm enough time to bounce back, which I learned to do in pro ball. I remember pitching in the state playoffs. I was throwing in the bullpen when I realized that I didn't have a fastball. The ball just wasn't popping, so I went with a lot of breaking balls. We talked about this after you signed me and after we got to be friends. You were glad because a lot of the scouts thought this guy was a junk baller rather than a power pitcher.

"Right before the draft, Jesse Flores with Minnesota, had me throw for him. I threw to a good friend of mine, George Adams. It was muddy that day. I had my parents' little Boston terrier with me. Jesse comes walking up with white pants on — I had never met the guy — he had called me on the phone and told me that he would meet me at Saguaro High School. And that damn dog goes running for this guy — Zip wouldn't hurt a fly — and jumps on this guy and smears mud all over his white pants. I'm thinking my chances are done now. I was scheduled to throw for the Pirates, but that fell through. Then you guys called me up.

"I met you guys at Saguaro. Here comes you and Larry — this big, burly guy — in his baseball uniform. Damned if he didn't look like a big league catcher! Boy, was I pumped! I remember you put the gun on me. I was throwing to Larry and I had been throwing my curveball 3/4, but wasn't getting completely over the top. Larry asked me if I could get my arm angle up just a little closer to my ear, which I did, and all of a sudden the break was more down than across. I could see that both you guys were pleased with that. When I was throwing hard, I asked you the velocity and you told me 87 mph. I knew that guys had been getting me in the low 90s, and I said, 'I know that I throw harder than that.' Remember that? I was bummed. I remember coming home and telling dad, and he said, 'I know what your problem is, you're gripping the ball too tight, trying to throw it through a wall.'

"I would have gone to Arizona State if I had gone to college. I used to go watch Kenny Jones when I was in high school. George Adams and I used to go there during batting practice and stand behind the fence and snag all the balls. Then we would go sit behind you and a bunch of other scouts and see how hard these guys were throwing.

"Coach Brock and Mrs. Brock came over in their Z and the license plates read: Brock 33, which I thought was awesome. They came over to the house and they were telling me that school is the only way to go, that I would get a full ride, everything would be covered, and if I had any problems in school I would get a tutor, and the only thing I would have to worry about would be baseball. I remember Mrs. Brock saying that they had tutors for every one of the players because the baseball schedule was tough and you had to miss some classes.

"Then the third of June rolled around and I got a call from you explaining that I had just been picked in the second round by the Cincinnati Reds. I hung up the phone, mom and dad were standing right there, and I told them. What a feeling!

"Coach Brock and Mrs. Brock came back over — they knew I had been drafted — and he told me that before I signed, to come back and talk with him. We got your offer and I went back and talked to him and he said, 'You've got to get at least $85,000. If you sign for less than that, then you're getting robbed.' I went back later and told him that I had signed. I figured I owed it to him.

"On the fifteenth I was on a plane to Billings, Montana. When I showed up, only two or three of us had signed out of high school, so we didn't know what the hell was going on. Guys were doing calisthenics, running line-to-lines, and being sure that their shoes were polished and their socks weren't too high. It was wild.

"The manager was Jim Hoff, who was a great guy, and the pitching coach was Marc Bombard, another good man. Billings was a great place to play. I remember we'd have our little workouts and Hoffy or Bomby would hit the ball back to the pitcher and he'd have to turn a double play, or throw it over to first base, or play the tough play and go cover first. The college guys had been through this stuff before, but I had never been through it, so I was giving it my all — throwing the ball as hard as I could. Bomby kept saying, 'Bone, take it easy. Just relax.' Finally, he got so mad at me that he said, 'Next time you throw it that hard, it's $25.' I wasn't trying to impress anybody; my adrenalin was flowing; I just loved what we were doing so much. The catcher and the first baseman weren't too happy with me, though.

"The college guys hung around together and I hung around with a guy from California, Doug Barba, who was also seventeen — two guys from the West. There was a little problem with the college guys. 'Bonus baby' was thrown out. Stuff like that. Not that they were trying to start anything, but just to where they got their little laughs from the guys behind them. I remember talking to my dad about this and he told me what to do. We were down in the bullpen one time — I can remember this like it was yesterday — and one of the guys on the team mouthed off and I just stepped right up and grabbed him by the jersey and said, 'I'm tired of catching all of this stuff from you, and if you want to settle it, let's settle right here and now in front of everybody.' From that day on everybody accepted me.

"I was wild. But I had a lot of tools. Both Bomby and Hoffy were real impressed with me. I wasn't worried about the hits I was giving up, I was worried about the walks. I was constantly behind in the count and had a hell of a lot of trouble getting my curveball over. They tried to change my delivery because I was having problems throwing the ball over the plate. But I don't think it was my mechanics, I think it was my make-up. I'm somebody who always gives a little more than I should, and it takes me a little while to settle in and realize how much I have to give to get by. They altered my mechanics a little bit, trying to get me to throw like Tom Seaver. They tried to get me to break over the knee with my arms and make my wind-up similar to his. At that time I was willing to try anything. At the end of the year I threw a one-hit shutout against Helena. I had 9 strikeouts and maybe 1 or 2 walks. I thought I was on my way.

"Later that fall I went out to California and pitched for Larry Barton, Jr.'s Reds team. I got a lot of help from Larry and there was no pressure. We were playing against good major colleges, so the competition was there. Eric Davis was on the team, Darryl Strawberry, big league pitchers like Frank Pastore and Joe Price, so I got the experience of playing with some really good players. You could work on things in a relaxed atmosphere, but it was still a baseball atmosphere. It was good.

"But I did find out I was short-arming the ball. I didn't even know what that meant. Larry said, 'Your arm is not extended out the way it should be.' Ed Roebuck, another scout with the Reds, had filmed me with his video camera against UCLA. So we worked on it. Then Roebuck filmed me again and we compared the two. And damned if Barton wasn't right. I was short-arming probably 8 or 10 inches.

"I think I was doing this because it was a conglomeration of my old wind-up, and the two or three different ones I was trying in Billings. If Michael (Jim's 7-year-old boy) gets into ball, I won't let anyone touch him. I think it just depends on a pitcher's body and his flexibility, and the way he is made to pitch. Give a young pitcher two or three years before you try to change him.

"I went into spring training in great shape, I was throwing the ball real good. Everyone was assigned to a different team and I was assigned to the Tampa team. There were tons and tons of guys in Reds uniforms. You did a lot of conditioning, a ton of running, you did a lot of throwing, there was a lot of instruction. It was a good experience. Twelve or fourteen days went by before you had your first game. You're away from home, you're on your own pursuing your dream, you're with a bunch of guys you don't know, and suddenly you realize you have turned into a man.

"I can remember you telling me that I was rated the second best pitching prospect in the Reds organization coming out of spring training that year.

"I pitched with Tampa in 1981. I was inconsistent. I started out 6-2, but I ended up petering out. Jim Lett was the manager. Marc Bombard was the pitching coach. Scott Breeden was also a pitching coach. I was getting instruction from both of them. I'm not making excuses, but one guy was telling me to try this, and the other guy was telling me to try something else. In the back of my mind I was still feeling what it used to be like to pitch.

"I remember Chief Bender, the Farm Director, calling me aside and saying, 'Don't worry about anything. There's no pressure. You're going to be in the big leagues for us one day. You remind me exactly of Frank Pastore. He had the same problems. He pitched well, then he would pitch lousy. It was all in his head. Just let it all go and just go out and do what you do best.' That made me feel good.

"I remember pitching against Vero Beach. I lasted two innings, they really hit me hard, I gave up six runs, I didn't get a strikeout, and I walked a ton of guys. The next time I faced them, I threw a one-hitter and struck out twelve. I couldn't fall into a rhythm. I was fighting against myself. The whole key to pitching is getting ahead, throwing strikes, and I couldn't do that consistently.

"I threw a fastball, curveball, and straight change. It took me three and a half years before I could throw the curveball over. It became a strikeout pitch. I think I gave up only three hits in all the years that I pitched on that curveball, and they weren't hits that somebody got ahold of and really hit it well.

"George Zuraw, a Reds scout, got me throwing 94 and 95 mph in Lakeland. He talked to me afterwards and encouraged me. He was a great guy. Larry Doughty, another scout with the Reds, was a great guy. He talked to me several times and said, 'Hang in there, things will work out.'

"At that point, in my mind, I wish they would have left me alone. Just give me a little bit of time to see if I could put it back together. One guy would say that I should stride out this far, one guy would say I am landing on my heel, one guy would say my arm was dragging. I had all that stuff in my head, thinking what I have to do in the middle of my delivery on a crucial pitch. What do you call it? Paralysis by analysis. It shouldn't be that way. It should be natural, just let the ball go.

"After the season, I went to the Instructional League. I pitched decent. That winter I ended up going back to California and I pitched for Larry again. He was very upset and asked me what they had done to me. I asked him what he meant. He said that I was short-arming the ball worse than ever. He got on the horn to Cincinnati and told them to leave me alone. After that, the word was out that I had squawked about all the attention and instruction I was getting. I could sense that they were upset with me.

"At spring training Harry Dorish started working with me. Bill Fischer, the big league pitching coach, saw me pitch and talked to me. He said that I had the best curveball that he had ever seen, that I was young and there was no reason why I couldn't make it. Everything was positive. Harry really tried to help me. He was from the old school where he'd throw a fastball right behind your ear if you looked at him wrong. That's the way he taught his pitchers — you've got to pitch inside. He was a gamer.

"I pitched at Cedar Rapids that year. It was a terrible year. I was 3-13. I was lost. It might have been the fact that I had been around a while and things just weren't coming. Harry Dorish was with me there and he was trying new things with me. I had Larry in California telling me to go back to the way I used to pitch, just be sure to extend my arm, and Harry was telling me different points. I didn't know how I was supposed to pitch.

"I did meet Lisa two months after we were there. She was very supportive. I had a shoulder to lean on. Actually, she was outstanding. It was a real tough time in my life and my career because I thought it was over with. I wasn't going to give up, but I thought the Reds might give up on me. I remember guys talking among themselves, wondering who was going to be released. That's a scary thing. I gave up college to play pro ball. It's like somebody has control of your life. Baseball is your life and all of sudden, no, you can't play anymore. My dream was always to be a big league pitcher, not for the money, just to pitch against the best.

"There was a lot of pressure, on and off the field. I can honestly say that I hung around with the right guys. You would see guys with all the talent in the world, but you knew they weren't going anywhere because they were hanging around with the wrong crowd and got mixed up in the wrong things. Especially the younger guys. There was some drugs, but there was a lot of booze. That was the thing to do, go out and get liquored up. Young guys get together, get away from home with a lot of time on their hands, and guys can get into the wrong things.

"Then I went back to the Instructional League and pitched great. They had backed off as far as giving me instruction, so I went back to my original mechanics that I had in high school. I pitched my way and I did great. But my velocity wasn't what it was. It was weird because I had been in the 90s in high school, Billings, Tampa, and in Cedar Rapids, but not as much in Cedar Rapids, 86 mph and once in a while in the 90s. At that time I wasn't worried so much about velocity, I was just trying to get my stuff together so that I could still make it. I went out to California and pitched a little bit for Larry and did well.

"I did well in spring training and broke camp with the AA team. I went to Waterbury, Connecticut. Jim Lett was the manager. He was strict but he was the kind of guy who had fun when it was time to have fun. And he knew me well. Dorish was the pitching coach. I had a mediocre year. I was still getting some pitching instruction but I was inconsistent. I have nobody to blame but myself. I don't know what it was. Near the end of the year I broke my hand and sat out for three weeks.

"They asked me to go to the Instructional League again and I did. I pitched there and I pitched well again. I pitched a little bit for Larry out in California that winter. I thought I'd get another shot at AA, but they put me back in Cedar Rapids.

"I think they had given up on me. You feel like an old man when they put you back with a bunch of young kids. This was going to be it — the last hurrah. Go out and pitch and have fun. All the pressures were gone. But when I got there I said to myself, 'Piss on this, I'm going to work my ass off, I'm not going have any of these guys mess with me, I'm just going to pitch, and I'm going to make it.'

"Jim Lett was the manager in Cedar Rapids. It was like he followed me wherever I went. My first couple of games were just brutal. In the second game against the Cardinals, Jimmy pulled me in the second inning. I had one out. I was walking down the tunnel from the dugout and there was a light there, and I just punched out the light. I went in and pounded on the Coke machine, ripped my uniform off, and jumped into the shower. All the guys could hear me because they were in the dugout. The next thing I heard was Jimmy Lett yelling and hollering coming up the tunnel to the showers. He said, 'What the hell is your problem?' I said, 'What the hell is my problem? I've been in this organization for four years and it's still the World Series. I'm out there trying. I can't get out of this hole if you pull me in the second inning. Let me get my brains beat in! Let me walk the ballpark! It's A ball! It's not the World Series!' He just looked me in the eye and turned and walked away.

"The next game — I was starting every five days — I went out and got in trouble. He left me out there. And I got out of it. From then on, Ed, I pitched great. I ended up with a 2.4 ERA, led the league in complete games, and was third in the league in strikeouts. This was the first year that I had put it all together. They had a neat scoreboard at Cedar Rapids. My name was going up there and it had never been up there for anything. It was showing that I was leading the league in this and that. I didn't have any pitching coaches doing anything with me. I was doing my own thing. I had 126 strikeouts in 125 innings, my hits were down, my walks were down. I received an award for most improved player. All the hard work had finally paid off.

"Greg Riddoch, the new Farm Director, had come down and said, 'Jimmy, we're really happy with you, we're really pleased that you've got it all going, and you're going to make a move here in another couple of weeks either to AAA or AA.' So Lisa and I went home and we boxed our things up. We were all excited. I didn't tell one player on my team. I thought, I'm not going to be Mr. Bragger, I'm just going to let it happen. We waited and waited and waited. Nothing. Not a damn thing! The end of the season came. Nothing. I was really disappointed. Like I said, I had struggled for so long, Ed, it was the first time in my career that I would have two balls and no strikes and I could throw my curveball over. Why is it all of sudden coming around? Is it luck? Am I going to be able to do the next game? And I did it the next game, and the next game, and the next game. All that hard work, all the disappointment, all the times I struggled didn't mean a damn thing because it had all jelled and I could pitch.

"I didn't go to the Instructional League. They said I had pitched enough innings and that I would be in AA or AAA next year. During the off-season I did help out at Saguaro High School. I helped the younger kids, I ran with them, and I conditioned myself. I was getting ready for the 1985 spring training and I was doing some long-tossing and it felt like I had some sand in my shoulder. That's exactly what it felt like. Nothing really hurt but it felt grindy and sandy. I would throw, feel it, and then it would go away. It was like that every day. I'd always go to Saguaro and throw against a wall. I'd work on my delivery — *my* delivery — and I could get to where I could hit any brick that I wanted to on the wall. But my arm just didn't feel right. There was pain when I threw hard. I thought, great, I just had a great year, I'm to the point where I can really go places, and now I've got this problem. I thought, hell, I'll just lay off and go to spring training and see what happens.

"So I went to spring training. We long-tossed the first couple days, played catch, did our P-F-P (pitcher-fielding-practice), then three or four days later we had to throw on the side for five minutes. We didn't have to throw hard, so I didn't feel any pain. I thought the problem was gone. Two days later you throw ten minutes. One day later fifteen minutes. Suddenly I started feeling the pain. I didn't tell anyone about it because, hell, I'm going somewhere, I'm going to make this club. But it was getting worse and worse. When I was sleeping I could feel the pain if I moved it wrong. Finally, I went to one of the trainers and told him that, hey, I've got a little stiffness — I never told him it was pain — in my shoulder. They gave me some anti-inflammatory pills and I took those like crazy. They saw that there wasn't any progress, so they had me take ten days off. They had me see a doctor in Tampa. He x-rayed my shoulder and diagnosed it as tendinitis. So he told me not to throw for two weeks. By that time spring training was about shot.

"They told me that they were sending me back to Cedar Rapids, and when my arm comes back, they'll move me up. I couldn't bitch. They could have released me right there if they had wanted to. I said fine. So we went back to Cedar Rapids. The arm wasn't getting any better. It even started to hurt when I was long-tossing. The trainer had me doing a bunch of exercises. I saw a doctor there who did an x-ray and said I had supraspinatus tendinitis. The supraspinatus is a muscle that goes across the front of the shoulder. He gave me some Motrin, or who knows what, I was on so many different types of medicine. He put me on a Cybex program for a month. It's a machine that has different connections so that it can work the right part of your body. As much force as you push towards it, it pushes that much force back. They tested my arm strength and my right arm was 40 percent weaker than my left. It's supposed to be the other way around. I worked on the Cybex machine every day, no throwing, and then I started throwing again and didn't feel any pain. But once I started to bear down, it was there again. So they diagnosed it again and said it was infraspinatus tendinitis. So they started working that muscle. I was on the Cybex again. It didn't get better. They told me to take a month off — no Cybex or anything. We're in the middle of the year by now. And I'm sitting and watching all these guys pitching. It sucked!

"We went on a road trip to Madison, Wisconsin. The key was if I could get by for three weeks without pain, then they would activate me. I was having major pain. I told the bus driver I would pay him if he drove me to a clinic. He was a great guy, so he drove me to the clinic and I signed myself in. I told a lady that I've got this racquetball tournament, just a bunch of us get together every year, we take our vacations and come down here and play racquetball. I also told her I'd been getting a cortisone shot every six months and I was due for another one. She told the doctor and the doctor gave me a cortisone shot. It didn't do anything. I threw that day. It was like he had shot me full of water.

"So, finally, I couldn't even long-toss. I told the trainer. They sent me to the University of Iowa where they did an arthogram. They shot dye in my rotator cuff to see if there was any leakage, which there wasn't. They said it was tendinitis and gave me some more medicine. It was the same old crap. I was thinking that these guys don't know what they're talking about. We went back to Cedar Rapids and tried another rehab program. It didn't work. They sent me back up to the University of Iowa and did a tomogram, which is very similar, except they shoot you full of dye and this great big machine goes in circles and takes pictures of your arm and shoulder at different angles. They said it looks like you've got some swelling in there, it's tendinitis, and you might have to lay off for the year.

"Well, about that time Riddoch comes into town. I'm sure my doctor bills are up there. He told me while I was dressing out in my locker that he would like to talk to me down in the bullpen. I thought, I'm released, I'm done. So I went down to the bullpen. He said, 'How you doing?' I said, 'I'm doing okay.' He said, 'What are your feelings about your arm?' I said, 'These guys I'm seeing don't know what they're doing. Greg, it's like I'm seeing a veterinarian.' He said, 'Jim, I don't think you have any right to say that. You're not qualified to make those decisions and they are.' He was negative. It was like he didn't have any feeling for what I was talking about. And he said, 'You know what I might suggest?' I said, 'What?' He said, 'That you might retire.' I said, 'What are you talking about? I've put all this time and effort into it. I just turned my career around last year and now I've got a little setback. I can work through it. What I need to do is see a real good doctor.' He said, 'Who do you want to see?' I said, 'I want to see Dr. Jobe.' He said, 'We don't see Dr. Jobe.' I knew damn well they did. I knew guys who had seen Dr. Jobe.

"So later I got on the phone and pressed him on it. I told him that I wanted to go see Dr. Jobe. He said that we don't send anyone there. I kept talking to him. I told him that I had seen four different doctors, and all of them are telling me four different things are wrong with my arm. One says supraspinatus, another infraspinatus, another fluid build-up. None of them seem to know. Just let Jobe take a look at it. He said fine.

"So we flew out to L.A. I had brought my records with me. He looked at all that stuff and said that I might have a problem right here, and pointed right in the capsule of my shoulder. He said that he would have to do an arthroscope, minor surgery, where he goes in and puts a camera in the back of my shoulder. I remember waking up and there was Lisa crying. I said, 'What's the matter?' She just started crying harder. She said, 'He found more wrong than he thought.' I said, 'What is it?' She said, 'Well, I'll let him tell you.' So a couple hours went by and he came in and said that he was really going to have to do some work. I didn't have to do it unless I wanted to. He said that the muscle in there was like hamburger and the shoulder was kind of separated. It's risky surgery and very new, but if I was willing to try it, he thought it could make my shoulder better. He said that the chances that I would pitch again were slim. I said, 'Let's do it.'

"We went back over to California a few weeks later and he ended up taking out a lot of chips that were floating around, that had broken off. He also found some bones in there that were growing and that's where I was feeling the pain. The shoulder had kind of separated and some pieces were floating around. So really while I was pitching and doing that Cybex stuff, I was tearing my shoulder up.

"Jobe saw the problem right away. He saw that the capsule was pulled away. Ed, the question I have in my mind, what if I had seen Jobe right away? It could have been just a chip. It could have been just a bone spur. What if I hadn't done the Cybex program? I have all these what-ifs.

"So he went in and basically tightened the joint up, and when I got out of there, my flexibility was zero. It's still not right. This was in November 1985. I was on rehab with small weights trying to stretch it out. I was hitting it hard. It was real painful. It would bring tears to my eyes but I could see progress. Lisa would help me every damn night. She'd pull on me and stretch that thing out. Jobe was amazed how much we had stretched it out.

"Surprise. The Baltimore Orioles drafted me in the professional draft that winter. They knew the situation. I was still in a sling when I was talking to them on the phone. I missed spring training. I joined them in Hagerstown, Maryland. They were good to me. They told me that they didn't want me to pitch an inning. Just see if I could be ready for next year. I went through some pain as far as throwing, but it wasn't pain like before. It was pain working through old scar tissue. I threw on the side, threw a lot of long-toss, did a ton of stretching, did some weight work, did a lot of running, then I'd shower and sit up in the stands and watch the games. And my arm was coming around, believe it or not. Near the end of the year I was throwing on the side and I felt it go. I ended up going back to see Jobe. He cut me open in the same spot and looked inside. He was amazed that I had gone as far as I did. He said that the joint was just trashed. He told me that I could never pitch again. So that was that.

"It was tougher than hell on me watching the Reds in the 1990 World Series. A lot of those guys are my friends, but a little part of me died inside. You see that and you realize that it's still there. It'll be there forever. That's when the what-ifs start coming into your mind. But I would do it all over again. The only thing I would change is as soon as I felt any kind of arm problem, I would go to the best doctor that I could, who I believe is Dr. Jobe, and maybe things would be different. It would have been cheaper going to the best right away anyway. But the last thing I want anyone to think is that I'm a whiner or moaner. Dad didn't bring us up to be that way. Everyone has their hard knocks in life. I'm just lucky enough to have Lisa, who helped me through everything, a great family, and good friends.

"I play in this semi-pro league. There are some ex-big leaguers in it, some ex-minor leaguers in it, and there are a lot of college guys who play in it. I play first base and I've learned to swing the bat. It's fun. But there would be times when we would need some pitching and I couldn't stay out of it. I still can't. I'd end up throwing a couple innings. Everything comes back to you. If I was 75 years old, and somebody put a ball in my hand and a batter up there, everything would come back to me. Your tools aren't there, but your mind and heart is. If somebody wanted to sign me to go play first base, I would go right now."

                              *   *   *

A scout always wishes he could draft players that come from families like the Pettibones. The odds are so against a player making it to the big leagues, that anything that can change those odds helps, and coming from a good family changes the odds because the player has a support system, roots, an anchor, something to hold onto when he confronts adversity.

I felt welcomed from the very first moment I walked into the Pettibone home. Dick and Penny Pettibone were genuinely hospitable people. Dick was quiet, serious, and full of questions. He was a man I trusted immediately. Penny was pretty and bouncy and very likeable. Both were greatly concerned about their son's future. Dick, Penny, Jim, and three older brothers and an older sister formed a tightknit family.

A few years later I was shocked when Jim told me that his dad had cancer. An operation followed. The cancer was remitted, but only for a while. Two heart-wrenching images stick in my mind from this period. One off-season I was watching Jim pitch from a mound he had built in his parents' back yard when I happened to glance over at the house and there standing behind the sliding glass door watching intently and holding hands were Jim's dad, and Jim's little, redheaded daughter, Mandy. One life ending, one life beginning.

I also can remember visiting the mortuary. The family was there, the casket was open, and Dick Pettibone was lying in the casket holding a baseball in his hands. On the baseball was written:

                    Thanks for everything, Dad.
                              Love,
                              Jim

                              *   *   *

Jim and Lisa Pettibone live in Chandler, Arizona, with their three children. Jim is an Operational Manager at Price Costco.

NOTABLE QUOTES

"Whoever said that New Mexico is

the Land of Enchantment was

easily enchanted."

— Rocky Bridges
Manager, Phoenix Giants

(This quotation from an Albuquerque newspaper almost caused an overflow crowd of angry New Mexicans to riot at a season opener in Albuquerque. Not the least bit intimidated, Rocky skipped out to hand the umpires his lineup card, and then skipped back to the dugout.)

The author conducting a tryout camp in Scottsdale, Arizona.
(EDWIN HOWSAM COLLECTION)

4

Tryout Camps

Over the years I have seen thousands of young men try out. A few have signed, some have become "follows," scores have received baseball scholarships from college coaches who were at the tryout camps, and all were allowed to have their moment on center stage.

It's physically impossible for a scout to see every player in his territory play. The tryout camp is the perfect vehicle for a scout to see the unseen player. Anyone can walk into one. But talk means nothing here, only performance and potential. The tryout camp is where boyhood dreams are put on the line.

Tryout camps are held for two reasons: (1) to sign players to professional contracts, and (2) to get leads on good young players whose progress can be followed in the future.

It isn't often that a future major leaguer is signed out of a tryout camp, but it can happen. Dan Driessen, a member of the Big Red Machine, was signed out of one.

Because of tryout camps in Las Vegas, I knew long before other scouts the abilities of Mike Morgan, Marty Barrett, Mike Maddux, and Mike's skinny little brother, Greg, who used to tag along. But it was more than just discovering physical talent, I got to *know* the players and their families.

A key word in baseball scouting is *speed*: running speed, bat speed, and the speed of a pitched ball. The tryout camp is designed to identify players who have these physical "tools."

I tried to maintain an age limit at the tryout camps from 15 to 22 years of age, but if anyone wanted to try out he (or she) could have at it.

After explaining to the players what I was looking for and what we were going to do, I ran all of them in a 60-yard dash, then threw everyone from his respective position, and after that had the pitchers throw to hitters. Gifted players stood out like wildflowers in the desert.

Some scouts cut players after everyone has run and thrown, and then organize a game with the better players. I didn't do that. Some of these players had driven more than 500 miles to attend one of my tryout camps; in addition, I didn't have the luxury of time in the Southwest because of the heat factor. It was 115° at the Scottsdale tryout camp in 1986. I certainly wasn't going to cut any player who had the desire to try out under those conditions.

The Cincinnati Reds wanted players to meet certain standards: run a 60-yard dash in 6.9 seconds or under, and throw a fastball around 90 mph. In short, I was looking for youngsters who could run and throw, hit the ball hard, and young pitchers who could throw hard.

However, only a fool sees the world in black and white. The same applies in baseball scouting. Nothing is carved in stone. There are too many successful big league players who couldn't measure up to an absolute standard.

For example, one of the best big league pitchers I ever saw had a 79 mph fastball. (Many high school pitchers can throw a 79 mph fastball.) But Randy Jones had a delivery so deceptive that when he threw his 79 mph fastball, it was like he was throwing 95 mph. I never saw so many *good* hitters chase balls outside the strike zone as they did against Randy.

And I certainly wouldn't lose interest in a young catcher just because he couldn't run 6.9 in the 60 — it's not that important for a catcher to run well — but he had better have a strong arm because you're not going to catch if you can't throw. Other factors besides position had to be considered: age, experience, competition, and climate. Baseball is a warm-weather sport; therefore, weather plays an important part in a player's development. Scouting a player in Utah is totally different from scouting a player in Southern California.

I've often wondered how I would have evaluated a young Pete Rose had he showed up at one of my tryout camps. Rose wasn't a "natural." Scores of his contemporaries in the major leagues had better baseball skills. They could run faster, throw better, field better, and hit a ball farther. Rose's physical assets were good vision, strong, quick hands, superb eye-hand coordination, excellent reflexes, great leg strength and good upper-body strength. But all of these attributes weren't apparent at 16 years of age. What nobody could have projected about Rose was his durability (he never got hurt), his love for the game, his willpower, his never-satisfied attitude, his narcissism, his holy quest for records, his work habits, and his baseball intelligence.

So how would I have graded Pete Rose at my tryout camp? Rose could run when he was young, so he would have caught my eye in the 60-yard dash. His arm and defensive abilities probably would have made me wince.

But his hustle, aggressiveness, and brashness would have stood out. He would have made good contact at the plate, but he wouldn't have shown much power. Pete Rose would have come away as a "follow" from the tryout camp.

In my tryout camp travels I've heard players speak French (Trois-Rivières, Québec), Spanish (El Paso, Texas), Mandarin (Taipei, Taiwan), pidgin English (Honolulu, Hawaii), and English with an Australian accent (Sydney, Australia).

As one might imagine, some funny, nutty, and poignant things have happened along the way.

One year when I arrived at the field in Las Vegas I was surprised to find a boy sleeping on the pitcher's mound. He said that there was no way he was going to miss the tryout camp.

Another time in Las Vegas, a catcher who said he was 21 years old (he was 30 if he was a day) told me that "I'm the best I've ever seen." I had to bite my lip to keep from laughing.

Quinn Marsh showed up at the tryout camp in Salt Lake City in June 1986. He was a right-handed pitcher from Bountiful, Utah. When he had graduated from high school two years before, he was 5 feet, 8 inches tall. A year later he was 6 feet, 4 inches tall. His fastball literally had gone from 60 mph to 90 mph. We took Quinn in the twenty-third round of the draft that year.

I nearly froze on May 24, 1980. We were holding a tryout camp in the Salt Lake City area. We had run everyone in the 60-yard dash, and Don Gust, our part-time scout in Utah, was hitting infield. Before he could finish, there were four inches of snow on the ground. Driving up the day before from Phoenix where the temperatures had already hit 100°, I was never so ill-prepared for a blizzard. I thought I had frostbite all over my body.

Once at a tryout camp at Phoenix College the temperature was well over 100°. Over 100 boys had showed up to try out. Unfortunately, the field had been watered just before the tryout camp started. I ran all the players in the 60-yard dash. After that — because of the heat and humidity — no one could do anything. They were all completely spent. I should have sent everyone home right then. It was so miserable that I kept praying that *I* wouldn't pass out.

During my scouting tenure with the Reds, I held 34 tryout camps in the Phoenix and Tucson areas. Not once did the temperature not reach at least 100° at every one of those tryout camps. I found out in a hurry which players wanted it and those who didn't. In 1986 when it reached 115° in Scottsdale, 117 players showed up to try out. One high school catcher stayed to the very end. He could hardly stand; he was on the verge of heat exhaustion. I'll never forget kids like him.

In Tucson, a little 45-year-old man with crazy Doc Holliday eyes tried out as a left-handed pitcher, but on my radar gun he couldn't break the speed limit (55 mph at the time), and the hitters were hitting rockets off him. (Get the married men out of the infield!) After he pitched, I thanked him for trying out and I told him that I wasn't going to be able to sign him, but he wouldn't take no for an answer. He told me that he had something that no Reds pitcher had. I asked him what that was. He gazed into my eyes and said, "*I* have a rubber arm."

A 64-year-old man once tried out in Santa Fe. I remember praying that he wouldn't have a coronary as he was running the 60-yard dash. He didn't but I could have timed him with a sundial instead of a stopwatch.

In June 1987 at Flagstaff, I conducted the only tryout camp that's ever been held in northern Arizona. Things got hectic because I was running it by myself. I had to get 81 players registered, talk to the players about what I was looking for and what we were going to do, do TV and newspaper interviews, measure off 60 yards, time everyone in the 60-yard dash (just as we started, the sprinklers in the outfield came on), grade everyone as I was hitting infield, use the radar gun on the pitchers, grade all the pitchers and hitters, keep track of the baseballs, bats, batting helmets, catcher's gear, and foul balls, and then talk to players and parents after the tryout camp.

I always had a good rapport with the media at tryout camps. Once a reporter, Thomas "Boomer" Ropp, tried out and wrote an amusing story titled "Why I'm Not in Cincinnati." He ended the story this way:

"Removing my cap, I walked away briskly from the diamond and into a field filled with irrigation water. I forgot all about baseball as my shoes sank slowly in the mud."

Some TV sportscasters tried out on camera. Some seriously, some as a spoof (where they tripped and fell down running the 60, misjudged fly balls, booted ground balls, struck out, etc.).

I once signed a black outfielder named Don Lyle out of a Phoenix tryout camp. He tried out in his stocking feet and had to borrow a glove because someone had stolen his spikes and glove right before the tryout camp began. He promptly went up to Billings, Montana, and nearly led the Pioneer League in hitting. But what I remember best about Don is that he used to write me the most beautiful letters. He would use a ruler on a plain piece of paper to make all the lines, and then he would painstakingly write with the neatest penmanship you ever saw. It must have taken him hours to write one letter. I cherish those letters.

In the summer of 1971 I was in Quebec City, Canada, probably the most charming, most European, and most historical city on the North American continent. I was assessing the baseball situation not only in *La Belle Province* but also in the Maritime Provinces. I was working on my itinerary when I received a letter. I read the letter once, and then again very slowly, savoring the contents. (The names used are not the real ones, except for mine.) The letter, written in longhand, read:

Friday

Dear Mr. Howsam,

  I understand that you are trying to locate potential big league players from Eastern Canada. Well I have two fellows that has all the potential my son is one & Johnny Dawson is the other. Young Jake was & still is a ace pitcher & Johnny is a real good catcher. Young Jake can run the bases in 4 seconds flat. I know he can make the majors & pitch right away & he would do this just for his room & board because he loves baseball & would play it day & night. Down here he also plays softball in order to get enough ball in. Johnny is also good ballplayer & could make the big times with a little polishing up, but I still insist that Young Jake is ready now with the proper coaching, he would be a super star because he was one ever since little league & humiliated senior teams since he was all of 14 yrs-old.

  You won't get much from the Nova Scotia Baseball Association because they don't know the war is over.

Thank You,
Mr. Jake Beliveau Sr.

  I wrote back thanking Mr. Beliveau for his letter, and told him I would be in his area in approximately three weeks and I would call on him at that time.

  The time passed quickly. First it was down to Montreal for an all-star game, up to Trois-Rivières to see some professional games, back up to Quebec City for some semi-pro playoffs, over to New Brunswick to catch the province's playoffs at Chatham and Moncton, ferrying to Prince Edward Island, back across to Nova Scotia and the long drive to Sydney via Cape Breton Island for a tournament, and finally to a place I shall call Lobster Bay.

  I called Mr. Beliveau at his home, but he was at the dentist's office. I passed the time at the harbor watching the lobster and cod boats unload their catch. I reached him with the next phone call, but he was so nervous that it was difficult to get instructions to his house. He came out the door wearing a Montreal Expos cap. We introduced ourselves, and drove to a softball field where Young Jake and Johnny were playing in a game.

It's hard to describe the position of importance that a scout assumes in certain rural communities. It's as if the clouds part and a deity walks forth. He's a novelty, a curiosity, a god. He can do anything, make any dream come true, bring fame and fortune.

Mr. Beliveau must have introduced me to everyone at the game. With the straightest faces imaginable, some of Young Jake and Johnny's friends told me everything the two of them had done in the softball game: how many hits, home runs, stolen bases, fielding gems, etc. I relished it all.

After the game we went to their baseball field, if one would choose to call it that. It had no backstop, the field sloped at a ten-degree angle, and the infield must have attracted rock collectors from miles around.

I measured off 60 yards and ran them twice. We had a vigorous infield practice. After that I had Young Jake throw his best stuff off the mound, and we finished up with some batting practice. Everything considered — baseball playing experience, the short Canadian season, lack of good coaching, and field conditions — they performed well but neither one was a prospect. Afterwards we discussed baseball at some length, even talking about Jim Bouton's book, *Ball Four*. I invited them to a tryout camp that we were going to have the following month at Trois-Rivières. It was time to go. I left with a good feeling. They had received a fair shot.

When I got back to Quebec City, I had this letter waiting. It read:

Sunday

Dear Ed,

It was really nice of you to work Young Jake and Johnny out but I feel like a heel. My wife gave me old hell for not asking you in the house, but I was so excited & pleased I guess I did everything wrong. If I knew you were here a day before I could of had you meet the press, radio & TV, our town father & maybe even had a party, but there's always another time, this old world isn't all that big.

All the boys says hello to you. I hope at your Tryout Camp Young Jake will get a chance at first base & outfield also. Then you can see him hit & steal bases.

If you like deer hunting let me know & I can take you to some real good places, now I mean deer, not beaver shooting, ha, ha.

Yours in Sports,
Jake Sr.

The day of the tryout camp arrived. All tryout camps are interesting, but this one would be even more so. It was to be conducted in both French and English.

To my surprise, Jake Sr. and five boys showed up, but it took some doing. They had had transmission problems along the way, and had slept two nights in the car. They had even watched an Expos game the night before in Montreal.

The tryout camp began. We put the 52 boys through their paces. Johnny Dawson fell into a dugout while chasing a foul ball, and he had to be taken to a hospital to have his right arm x-rayed.

The second day of the tryout camp started on time, but where were Jake Sr. and the boys? Young Jake and Johnny straggled in about two hours late. Some drunk had gone through a red light, smashing into the Beliveau's car. Everyone had gone to the hospital. Young Jake and Johnny had been released and had walked more than a mile to the park. Jake Sr. had hurt his neck and was having it x-rayed. He and the other boys showed up an hour later. His neck was so stiff that he could hardly turn it.

I put Young Jake on the mound. Johnny insisted on catching him. I refused at first but finally acquiesced after Johnny proved he could move his right elbow, which was now swollen to the size of a grapefruit. While Young Jake was pitching, Jake Sr. would yell at me and laugh. He was saying things like, "Hey, Ed, do you see Bob Gibson out there on the mound?" Have you ever seen a man laugh who isn't laughing, but who is deadly serious? Mr. Beliveau was desperate.

The tryout camp ended. Another scout and I talked to Young Jake about trying to find him a college baseball scholarship. This didn't mollify the disappointment in his eyes. Everyone was very quiet. We gave them each a new ball and they asked us to autograph them. When it was time for them to go and they got into their damaged car, I searched for words, not knowing what to say. What could you say to people who would drive well over a 1,000 miles, who couldn't afford it, who had had their car and their bodies smashed, but most of all who had had their dreams shattered? The only thing I could say was that I was sorry, really sorry. As they drove off waving, all I could think about was that incredibly stupid statement in *Love Story*: "Love means not ever having to say you're sorry."

The author with Norm Cockerell (#8) and Mike Klinger (#11) on a windy day in Melbourne, Australia.
(EDWIN HOWSAM COLLECTION)

5

Aussie Baseballers

In 1962 an American baseball official — who I'll kindly let remain anonymous — got off an airplane in Sydney and asked a taxi cab driver to take him to Perth.

It would have been an expensive fare, since Perth is some 2,000 miles from Sydney. This embarrassing anecdote isn't surprising. Few Americans, who are notoriously poor geographers, could identify Australia on a blank world map or name its capital.

Yet Americans and Australians genuinely like each other. One can slide in and out of both societies without much difficulty. We have much in common from our English heritage, and we are both relatively young countries with frontier experiences.

But America and Australia were founded in direct contrast; whereas America was founded by those seeking freedom, Australia was founded by those relinquishing theirs. In the beginning, the jail, the whip, and the noose shaped the Australian experience. For a brilliant account of Australia's brutal founding, read Robert Hughes' *The Fatal Shore*.

It's difficult to overestimate the importance of sports in Australian life. As Geoffrey Blainey relates in his book, *The Tyranny of Distance*, Australia emerged in the nineteenth century as one of the most sports-crazy nations on earth. Two factors caused this. First, Australia was a man's land, a society dominated by young men because there was a dearth of women. (Females didn't become as numerous as males until World War I, and only then because so many men were fighting in Europe.) Second, working conditions had changed enough by mid-nineteenth century to allow more leisure time. Thus, unmarried men had the time and money to pursue sports.

According to *The Australian Encyclopaedia*, baseball was first played in Australia in 1886. Just before the turn of the century, an Australian team ventured abroad and played 26 games in America, but this tour was reported to have been "a disaster, financially and otherwise."

In 1914 the New York Giants and Chicago White Sox played a series of exhibition games in Australia. Twenty years later a national championship tournament — the Claxton Shield — was established for senior players. Another milestone occurred in the summer of 1952 when night baseball was introduced by the South Australian League in Adelaide. But the 1970s was the pivotal decade for Australian baseball. Great leaps forward were made. In 1971 Australia was accepted into the Baseball Federation of Asia and began international competition. National championships were held for the first time in 1972 for Under 13, Under 15, and Under 18 age divisions.

The rise of baseball in Australia, however, hasn't been on one constant ascending line during its first century of existence. The world wars, lack of money, lack of playing fields, lack of competent coaching, the "tyranny of distance," and competition with cricket have plagued the game at one time or another.

Cricket, which is — shock — the national sport of Australia, has been a real thorn in baseball's side. This endless game (a final result may take *days*, not hours), which is as exciting as watching artificial turf grow, once relegated baseball to being played in the winter.

Today, though, baseball is alive and well in Australia. There are more than 400,000 Aussie baseballers from age six to the seniors. Tee Ball, a wonderful, action-packed, easy-to-play game, has burst upon the scene and caught the fancy of Australian boys and girls everywhere.

There have been six Australian players who have played in the major leagues. Joe Quinn, a second baseman, played and managed for several teams for 17 years and retired in 1902. Craig Shipley, a middle infielder, played for the Los Angeles Dodgers in 1986, and resurfaced with the San Diego Padres in 1991. Four other Aussies have played in the majors since 1992: Milwaukee Brewers left-hander Graeme Lloyd and catcher Dave Nilsson, San Diego Padres right-hander Mark Ettles, and New York Yankees right-hander Mark Hutton.

I traveled to Australia four times. Three times as a Reds scout on assignment: December 1976, January 1978, and January 1979. The fourth time, in January 1981, I paid my own way and took my ten-year-old son, Erik, with me.

By that time the Cincinnati Reds had abandoned scouting in Australia. This happened because there had been a "changing of the guard" at the top when Dick Wagner took over as president in February 1978, and because the farm director, Sheldon "Chief" Bender, had never supported the concept of scouting in Australia.

Although many things have changed in the past 18 years, my opinion of the value of scouting in Australia hasn't changed at all. Let me quote from my first report to Joe Bowen:

There have been individuals representing major league organizations in Australia before, and there are individuals in Australia today who represent certain major league clubs, but there never has been a scout who traveled so extensively, seen so much baseball at the top level, and met so many important baseball officials as I did on my recent trip to Australia. At times I felt like one of the great explorers exploring virgin territory. I literally have seen more of Australia than most Australians.

It is difficult to contain my enthusiasm. If we play our cards right, Australia can become almost exclusive Cincinnati Reds' property. We have gotten there "firstest with the mostest." It's as if we have opened a new baseball frontier. Imagine having first pick of a country of 13 million, which speaks English, has no restrictions on signing players, has officials whose passion for baseball must be seen to be believed, whose countrymen are probably the most dedicated sportsmen in the world, and where there is an explosion of baseball activity not only on the international scene but also at the pee-wee level. On the other hand, it must be admitted that baseball is a minor sport in direct competition with cricket, the national sport. But it is inevitable — maybe not today or tomorrow, but sometime in the future — Australia will produce its share of big league ballplayers.

On that first trip in December 1976 I accompanied a Florida high school all-star team. The team played two games in five states (New South Wales, Western Australia, South Australia, Victoria, and Queensland): one game against the state's Under 18 all-star team and one game against the Australian Under 18 all-star team.

Since Australia is nearly the size of the United States (excluding Alaska), we did a fair bit of traveling, and because Australia is the driest of all continents, the major population centers are on or near the coast. Our itinerary took us from Sydney to Perth to Adelaide to Melbourne to Brisbane.

We were treated with extraordinary hospitality wherever we went. I not only watched a lot of baseball, but I saw the Sydney Opera House, black swans in Perth, and a winery outside of Adelaide; I rode the trams in Melbourne, body surfed near Brisbane, and much more.

There are many fascinating things about Australia, but the one that confronts you first is the language. I can remember drinking a beer in a club after a game in Sydney and listening to an Aussie tell a joke. I might as well have been in Budapest, for I could understand very little of what the man was saying. But I was playing along and smiling from time to time, and I laughed when the others did at the end of the joke. It took a while to get used to the accent, different expressions, and idioms.

Of course, everything is relative. When I was in Australia, the Aussies didn't have an Australian accent, *I* had an American accent. The expressions and idioms I used were sometimes new and strange to them. When I didn't understand something, I would say, "Run that by me again." They would laugh and ask me what "run that by me again" meant. A different meaning for a word can cause a hilarious misinterpretation. The Aussie baseballers who first traveled to the United States thought they had discovered heaven on earth when the American girls watching the game told them that "they would root (make love) for the whole team."

In another setting, there was no misinterpretation, but the result was still hilarious. I was with some Australian baseball coaches drinking beer at a discotheque in Melbourne when a very pretty bird (girl) walked by. One of the coaches said to her, "Hey, Luv, have you ever tripped over a branch?" She stopped, turned around, and said, "What? What are you talking about?" And he said, "Well, then, how about a root?" I almost fell down on the floor I was laughing so hard.

Here are some expressions that one might hear at a baseball game in Australia:

> ground = field
> side = team
> stones = if a player weighs 12 stones, he weighs 168 pounds (14 pounds equal 1 stone)
> glorious = e.g., that was a glorious pitch
> lovely = e.g., he has a lovely arm
> right; she's right = okay
> barrack = root (Nice girls *don't* root for the whole team in Australia.)
> she'll be apples = things will be fine
> nil = zero; e.g., the score is five to nil
> it'll be mothballs = the season will be over
> spot on = accurate; e.g., the throw was spot on
> push them in = drive runners in
> equalizing run = tying run
> carnival = tournament
> good on you = good for you
> digs = inning

going off tomorrow = pitching tomorrow
spotter; talent scout = baseball scout
query an umpire = question an umpire's decision
no worries = no problem
reckon = believe or think
fair dinkum = e.g., I reckon he's fair dinkum (genuine).

In the newspaper one might read an account of the game peppered with phrases like: "a dazzling pitching display," "he dispatched a massive home run," "they squared the game," "lethal pitching," and "irresponsible batting."

Once a P.A. announcer made these comments during a game:

"There's an interesting story making the rounds about the next hitter. It seems he rode his motor bike all the way from Tenant Creek to Melbourne, some 1900 miles away. Here he is, ladies and gentlemen, Easy Rider Jim Ford." (Laughter.)
Someone shouts from the crowd, "And he doesn't have any brains either." (More laughter.)

"He was caught off in no man's land." (After a player was caught off first base and tagged out.)

"Tasmania's defense is steady." (After the shortstop made a good play.)

In the bottom of the 5th inning, the score was:
Tasmania   1
Queensland   0
"If you are one of those who like a fast game, then this is a good game."

"Up to this point the pitchers have been on top of the batters."

"Tasmania is capitalizing on a bit of uncertainty." (After Queensland's second baseman made an error.)

"Obviously that one didn't tickle." (After a pitched ball hit the hitter, who was in obvious pain.)

"He's giving the left field line a punishing." (After a line drive hit down the left field line was foul by inches.)

"Someone better move the car that's obstructing a footpath, or else the demons will book you." (If you don't move your car that's blocking a sidewalk, the police will give you a ticket.)

One night I was watching a senior game in Melbourne, and there was a pick-off play and the first baseman tagged the runner hard on the bun. Instantly a loud voice pierced the air, "Kinky!" Then another voice, "Don't touch your toes, mate!" Another one, "Make them take separate showers!" And another, "Don't bend over for soap, mate!"

How do the Aussies show their displeasure with umpires? One man who disagreed with a call yelled, "Rubbish, you animal!" Another fan sang out, "You should have gone home before the game started, mate."

Actually, to be fair, the Australian attitude toward umpires in particular and authority in general is quite different from the American attitude. It's uncommon for Aussie coaches, players, or fans to get on or argue with an umpire. If someone does, you can be sure that it's a "learned" trait. The Australian nature is to play on, not complain.

Aussie baseballers have their own peculiar characteristics. After watching a number of games, it struck me that there were almost no switch-hitters in Australia, but there were many left-handed throwers/right-handed hitters. One rarely sees these when scouting in America.

One of the more interesting features of Australian society is the tradition of mateship. Mateship — strong, healthy male friendships — dates back to the lonely and monotonous life in the harsh bush, where there were no white women, where men had to rely on and trust one another.

Team sports forge strong bonds anyway, but this is especially true in Australia where mates stick together, never wanting to let another mate down. This doesn't mean, though, that Aussies never criticize one another. On the contrary, Aussies are more open, more candid, and more willing to accept criticism than us "bloody Yanks". Win or lose, Aussies celebrate or console over a few beers.

When I first went to Australia I was hoping to discover an aboriginal Willie Mays. But those hopes were soon dashed. I seldom saw an Aborigine play baseball — never at the senior level — and the ones who I saw play weren't good ballplayers.

I rarely heard an Aussie speak out in support of the Aborigines. This silence spoke volumes; the feelings run deep. These two alien cultures and peoples — European and native — clashed from the beginning over the land.

The Australian experience with the Aborigine, like the American experience with the Native American, hasn't been very pretty. Bullets, diseases, lies, and alcohol have played an enormous part in both histories. European technology triumphed, not humanitarian values. Today, many of the same problems exist for both native peoples.

One day I was jogging in a small, hilly park that overlooked downtown Brisbane. As I jogged I could catch glimpses of the buildings through the leaves on the trees. I react to certain colors, so I especially enjoyed the flaming orangish-red flowers in the garden beds and the brilliant white flowers growing in the lush, green treetops. Sweat poured out of me as the subtropical sun stoked its fire. A cleanup man was picking up empty liquor bottles around an unoccupied park bench. Farther down, four tough-looking Aborigines were passing a bottle around. The heavy smell of liquor permeated the air. I was apprehensive. Suddenly one of the Aborigines said "Hi" and waved. I returned the "Hi" and the wave. His friendly gesture made me feel good. I picked up my pace a bit and the flowers in the gardens and treetops looked brighter as I jogged around the park again.

One thing that amused me about Australian baseball was the state rivalries. This could be observed in national competitions on the field and petty politics off the field. One coach from Queensland told me:

— in Victoria they ask: Who are you?
— in New South Wales they ask: What are you?
— in Queensland they ask: How are you?

It was quite astonishing and very refreshing to find the fanatical devotion and sheer love of baseball in Australia. For example, Tony Branigan, a coach in Western Australia, was a true baseball nut. His apartment was one large collection of baseball memorabilia. He said he had read each of his baseball books at least two dozen times. As one of the coaches of an Australian all-star team that had toured Florida in the spring of 1976, Tony not only kept every room key where he stayed, but he could not sleep the night before when he found out that he was going to see his idol, Johnny Bench, play in a spring training game. Naturally, Tony's nickname was JB.

Baseball is played through a club system in Australia, not through the school system. One doesn't scout high school and college baseball teams because they don't exist.

We have nothing in America that compares to a "club". Clubs run the gamut from the small to the all-encompassing. A club may provide lifetime involvement, the focal point of individuals and families, social as well as athletic. I visited one club in Sydney that had a nightclub, slot machines, movies, and offered group travel abroad. Some clubs drip with tradition: ivy-covered buildings, hallowed halls with squeaky, polished, wooden floors, old men peering down from old photographs wearing club ties worn with club blazers adorned with club crests.

I was very impressed by the Australian baseball officials I met. They were a group of men bonded together by their love of the game, and driven by their will to compete successfully at the international level. They also supported the game out of their own pockets at considerable expense.

I got to know three men well: John Anderson, Lyn Straw, and Ross Straw. John Anderson, President of the Australian Baseball Council, was the guiding force. Anderson was one of those rare individuals who combined keen intelligence with common sense. When John Anderson talked, everyone listened.

Are there two people anywhere on this planet who love the game of baseball more than the Straw brothers? Lyn Straw was the coach of the dynastic Victorian (The Big Blue Machine) junior team. He was a great teacher. Lyn actually listened to what other people had to say. A bright, splendid fellow.

Ross Straw was a big, aggressive man. He made things happen. Ross wore several different hats for Australian baseball, and he never lost sight of the long-range goals. It was great fun to be with Ross. He had a superb sense of humor and a magnetic personality.

In January 1978 I signed two Australian players. Neither was an outstanding prospect, but both were signable players. It was important to get the ball rolling.

Bob Nilsson was from Brisbane, Queensland. He was 17 years old when he signed. I had seen him catch, pitch, play the outfield, and third base. He was a big, powerful, raw-boned boy who didn't have the classical pitcher's physique, but who threw hard and had some movement on his fastball the only time I saw him pitch. He didn't know anything about pitching, but I considered this to be a plus. At least he hadn't developed any bad habits. If he couldn't make it as a pitcher, then he had a chance as a catcher because of his arm strength, build, and power. The last thing I wrote on his Newly-Signed Player Information Sheet was "Be Patient."

Paul Elliott was a catcher from Sydney, New South Wales. He was 21 years old when he signed. He was big, strong, rugged, and had a major league arm. His hands were okay. Paul was quiet off the field but a real take-charge player on the field. His bat wasn't a plus, but he showed occasional power.

I ended my February report to Joe Bowen by saying, "We're in great shape in Australia." Life is capricious. Four months later both players had been released.

In early June I was awakened at six o'clock by a telephone call from Chief Bender. He had never called that early before. He said that the two Australian players were going home because they hadn't shown much ability and because they *wanted* to go home. I was stunned. I was angry at Chief for releasing Nilsson and Elliott so soon without giving them a fair chance, but I was furious at the players for quitting.

Our scouting program in Australia died the moment the two players were released, but it wasn't a death with dignity. It was a slow, ugly death. I didn't learn the truth until I ran into Paul Elliott the following January in Australia when he asked me why he had been released. I asked him incredulously, "You mean you didn't ask to be sent home?"

The truth, of course, was that the new regime for the Reds wasn't interested in scouting in Australia. Like anything else, baseball has a few men of vision and many others who are blind.

Other changes were occurring as well. Another club was making its presence felt. Fred Claire (now the general manager) of the Los Angeles Dodgers was mixing business with a vacation to Australia. Fred had seen the Claxton Shield and Under 18 national tournaments. He told some Australian baseball officials at dinner — I happened to be present — that the Dodgers would start sending scouts and wanted to know if they would be interested in having Walter Alston travel there as a visiting instructor.

In recent years other clubs have signed players from Australia. In fact, the Nilsson story doesn't have an entirely sad ending. I was scouting the Arizona Instructional League in the fall of 1987 when I came across the name of a Dave Nilsson from Australia on the Milwaukee Brewers roster. Before one of the games I asked Dave if he were related to Bob Nilsson, and he said he was his younger brother. We had a good, long talk.

Like Bob when he signed, Dave was only 17 years old, but I was impressed by this young, left-handed hitting, redheaded catcher. He had an excellent stroke and eye for a young hitter. He had enough arm strength and size to play this difficult position. But the most impressive thing about him was that he *loved* to play baseball. I looked for good things to happen to young Dave. (He was called up by the Milwaukee Brewers on May 18, 1992.)

It's a small world, mate.

The author (right) with his brother, Robert Howsam, Jr.
(SARA HOWSAM)

6

A Day in the Life of a Minor League GM

Robert Howsam, Jr., General Manager, Denver Zephyrs, AAA

*   *   *

Robert is my older brother by two years. Big brothers come in handy sometimes. When we were little guys he prevented a crazy kid in the neighborhood from throwing me down a manhole. Later when we were in high school, we worked in the summers for Sturgeon Electric. The work was hard — digging ditches and using a jackhammer all day long. Sometimes after work we would go swimming to cool off. One evening we were swimming and I developed severe cramps in both legs and headed for the bottom like a rock. Bobby saw me on the bottom, dove, and pulled me out of the water.

When I was 6 years old, I started playing baseball on a team called the Bombers. I found out rather early about the difficulty of hitting a baseball, so I recruited Bobby to help me out. I had him get behind the screen and tell me when to swing at the ball. I can still hear him yelling, "Swing!"

I recall another time when I was maybe 8 or 9 years old, and I came home and discovered that my brother had locked himself in the bathroom and was crying. I knocked on the door and asked him what was wrong. He was crying so hard that he could hardly tell me that in the game he had pitched that morning, he had given up a hit and hadn't pitched a no-hitter.

Bobby was a fine hitter. He led the city of Denver in hitting his junior year in high school. He could knock the cover off the ball. I also remember when he knocked himself out by running into a fence while practicing for a high school baseball all-star game.

So what's Robert like? He's intense, ambitious, intelligent, opinionated, energetic, conscientious, and he eats like a truck driver.

*   *   *

Here's a day in the life of a minor league GM:

June 27, 1989

7:22 a.m.
Jogs around Cheesman Park.

8:40 a.m.
Leaves home for Mile High Stadium.

9:00 a.m.
Chairs staff meeting in his office with the ticket manager, public relations director, stadium operations director, sales director, and business manager. All discussion focuses on the Annual Fireworks Spectacular, scheduled for July 1. They're hoping for a crowd of 40,000.

9:47 a.m.
Discusses Synagogue Group Night news release to *Intermountain Jewish News* with Jon Puskin. Robert wants to be sure Andy Cohen's name is used in the news release. The enormously popular Cohen spent five seasons (1951-54 and 1958) as the Denver Bears field manager. Robert and Jon also decide that as part of the pre-game activities, each Denver area synagogue will be represented by a child who gets to visit the dugout, and who will receive an autographed ball and a souvenir Z's baseball cap.

10:02 a.m.
Calls Bryan Burns in the Commissioner's Office to discuss why Major League Baseball won't allow the International League and the American Association to televise their championship series in September.

10:16 a.m.
Calls Richard Campos of the American G.I. Forum's Veterans Outreach Program to offer free tickets to homeless Vietnam vets.

10:30 a.m.
Meets with representatives of the Police Department, Sheriff's Department, and Fire Department to work out details for the Second Annual Safety Night on July 13, which will include a round robin softball tournament among the three departments before the Zephyrs game. Members of the winning team will receive a Certificate of Appreciation which allows each team member

free transportation to the County Jail, one free night's lodging, room service, and a room with a view.

11:12 a.m.
Gregg Browning drops by to get a donation or gift from the Zephyrs for a NFL Alumni golf tournament. Browning, now retired, was one of Robert's football coaches at East High School. Robert ends up taking Coach Browning to a Mexican restaurant for lunch. They discuss happy remembrances: pep rallies, a state playoff game in 1960, funny stories, people then and now.

12:30 p.m.
Rushes to KUVO-89.3 FM, a jazz station, to do a live interview with David Nash. KUVO is in the midst of a membership pledge drive and "a celebration of the summer solstice." David, a baseball buff, lets Robert, a jazz buff, select the music for the next hour. Wedged in between glorious, soul-penetrating sounds from Les McCann, Eddie Harris, David Sanborn, and Pat Metheny, Robert answers questions about the Zephyrs and Fireworks Night.

I'm sitting next to Robert as he's talking and, unexpectedly, David starts asking me questions too. Before I know it, Robert and I are having a spirited exchange, debating whether or not Pete Rose belongs in the Hall of Fame. Robert takes the position that Rose belongs in the Hall of Fame; like any good brother, I take the opposite position, saying that the only hall Rose belongs in is the Hall of Shame. I'm sure this is exactly what the jazz listeners wanted to hear on their radio station.

1:51 p.m.
Peeks in on a tryout camp at Mile High Stadium being conducted by "Dirty Harry" Smith, a scout with the Milwaukee Brewers.

2:00 p.m.
Meets with Tim Shafer of KOOL-1280 AM radio to discuss Fan Appreciation Week, which will be held in August. It might be a baseball first: fans are selected to fulfill a carnival of baseball fantasies such as fantasy ground crew member, fantasy bat boy and bat girl, fantasy play-by-play announcer, fantasy color commentator, fantasy photographer, fantasy sports writer, fantasy national anthem singer, etc.

3:45 p.m.
Goes to City Hall to hear an in-depth presentation by Ron Straka, Urban Designer, comparing two baseball stadium sites near downtown Denver —

the Five Points site and the Central Platte Valley site. Everything is evaluated, from the earth's soil contamination to the micro-climate overhead. Topics like traffic access, land acquisition/cost, community acceptance, environmental concerns, and economic impact are broken down into minute detail.

5:17 p.m.
Shows the Zephyrs manager, Dave Machemer, and the pitching coach, Jackson Todd, the new batting cage behind the left field fence. Afterwards Robert chats with some of the players in the clubhouse.

5:42 p.m.
Norm Clarke, a reporter for the *Rocky Mountain News,* comes into Robert's office and reads a story hot off the wire that a witness has tied Pete Rose to drugs. Robert is shocked. The Pete Rose affair has baseball by the throat.

7:05 p.m.
Watches a crowd-pleasing game between the Zephyrs and the Indianapolis Indians. The Zephyrs fall behind early, but come back to win the game in the bottom of the ninth by a score of 6 to 5. The momentum changes in the third inning when the Zephyrs pitcher, Tom Filer, knocks down the Indians second baseman, Junior Noboa, who is hitting .396. Noboa bails out badly on the next two pitches — sliders away — and then meekly pops up. He has been humiliated; he has shown fear. He throws his helmet hard into the dugout. Later in the game, Jimmy Jones, the Zephyrs catcher, is hit in the side by a fastball. A brawl almost ensues. It's an intense, exciting game.

10:49 p.m.
Talks in the parking lot with Norm Clarke and Jay Mariotti, also a reporter with the *Rocky Mountain News*, about the breaking Pete Rose story.

11:03 p.m.
Leaves Mile High Stadium for home.

*   *   *

Robert spent eleven years as an advertising executive in New York City before joining the Cincinnati Reds as Vice President, Director of Marketing in 1983. He worked there for two and a half years before he was hired by John Dikeou, the owner of the Denver Zephyrs, to run the team as President and General Manager, and to help him obtain a major league team.

He was with the Zephyrs five years. Unfortunately, Robert had picked the wrong horse to ride to the big leagues, since Dikeou's commercial real estate business was suffering through the Colorado recession and bank foreclosures forced him out of being a contender for a team.

Until recently Robert was Associate Executive Director for the Colorado Springs Fine Arts Center. Now he's doing many things: sports marketing, a marketing consultant with a telecommunication company in Florida, and the Executive Vice President of the Colorado Springs World Arena.

                              *   *   *

Interview — October 15, 1994

Looking back, what did the experience of being a minor league GM mean to you?

From a personal standpoint, it was a unique cyclical experience. As a kid I had worked for the Denver Bears and watched games at Bears Stadium, then I traveled 2,000 miles away and spent a lot of my life away from this and then I returned years later. The stadium was different, of course, but it was still the same place. It brought me back to an earlier stage of my life.

Professionally, I was only interested in being a minor league GM because of the major league potential.

What were some of the good things and bad things about the job?

One of the good things about the job was that I got to know a lot of fans — people who really cared about something. It also made me feel like I was part of a team, that there was a common bond with people all over the city. Being on that team was very satisfying, and I had a chance to be in a position where I could make decisions that had some impact.

Bad things about the job? The long hours and being in a monstrous stadium with thousands of tons of concrete. It could be a lonely place too.

Are you still involved in baseball?

Well, I'm not part of the direct operation, but I am Dante Bichette's sports marketing agent. That means I get him sponsorships, speaking engagements, do a lot of PR work for him, work up charity programs around him, and do a lot of the leg work for him. In short, I try to enhance his image as the All-American boy who is happy to be playing in Denver for the Colorado Rockies.

I'm also the major league baseball operations consultant for a group that is trying to get a team for the Washington, D.C. area. I've been working on their major league expansion application, advising them on how to proceed, and emphasizing to them the importance of having a first-class stadium.

Did you ever think that major league baseball would be so successful in Denver?

Not to the degree that it has been. I thought that they could draw three million people, and of course they've exceeded that easily. It just shows what the people of Colorado can do when they get behind something.

What's your opinion about the strike?

Unfortunate. It seemed inevitable with the direction baseball was going. Always working under the same system that causes a great deal of tension and disagreement.

How do you feel about baseball's antitrust exemption?

I think it's been a crutch for baseball, and I think part of it may be at the root of why baseball has so many labor problems. On the other hand, I'm concerned about what will happen to the minor leagues if the antitrust exemption is removed.

What will baseball be like in 25 years?

I certainly see baseball going international, heading south to Latin America. I can see a team in Mexico City, maybe in Havana, possibly in Caracas. Latin America is a huge, untapped market full of baseball-crazy fans.

NOTABLE QUOTES

"*I **must** be at a ballpark. I hate to say it but it's my fix — if I don't see baseball every day, then I feel rotten.*"

— Joe Maddon
Minor League Manager, California Angels

"*I'd pay to hear myself sing in the shower.*"

— Bob Fontaine, Sr.
General Manager, San Diego Padres
(and a big fan of country-western music)

Jerry Macias
(EDWIN HOWSAM COLLECTION)

7

South of the Border

Baseball people are very competitive. On the field, in the front office, and in the search for players. Scouts for the Cincinnati Reds during the glory years of the Big Red Machine had to accept the fact that we weren't going to get the top picks in the draft, so we had to hustle and scramble to come up with good ballplayers in the lower rounds. We enjoyed the challenge.

I was lucky to work with two exceptional scouting directors, Joe Bowen and Larry Doughty.

I got to know Joe when we traveled to Taiwan together. He was gregarious, stubborn, witty, smart, hardworking, and a dedicated baseball man. You didn't ever try to put anything over on Joe, and if it came to negotiating anything with him, forget it. He'd be two jumps ahead of you every time.

Larry was quiet, intelligent, a great listener, easy to talk with once you got to know him, a student of baseball, a hard worker, and had a dry sense of humor. He greatly cared about his scouts; he'd back you all the way. I got to know him after my scout car broke down — transmission problems — outside of Wickenburg, Arizona. We had been in Las Vegas looking at a pitcher, and we were on our way to watch Arizona State play. We got towed into Phoenix, rented a car, and did get to see part of the Arizona State game.

For most of my scouting career with Cincinnati, there was a sense of team within the scouting staff. This teamwork approach came from the top and filtered on down.

This was important because it made much of the unpleasantness of scouting palatable. The emphasis was where it should be — on the success of the major league team and on what type of draft "we" had, and not on who signed whom, or how come he got so many players in the draft and I didn't? Nothing poisons a scouting staff more quickly than backbiting, boasting, cliques, and petty jealousies.

Scouting the outstanding and the poor players is easy. What's difficult is to find good players in the gray area. George Zuraw, a great scout who scouted Florida for the Reds, felt the best scouting jobs were done between the fifth and the tenth rounds. I wouldn't argue with that. Fine players like Tim Raines, Dave Steib, Steve Sax, Fred McGriff, and Terry Pendleton have all been taken somewhere between the fifth and tenth rounds.

Every scout has to accept certain things. Rarely does he ever get the players that he would like in the draft. It can be frustrating and discouraging. And in some years he's shut out all together. Larry Doughty told me that when he was scouting a territory for the Reds, he went three straight years without getting a player in the draft. I also got shut out one year. Drive all those miles, see all those games and players, write all those reports, hold all those tryout camps, be away from home for all those days, and not get *one* player in the draft. That's tough to swallow.

During my 17 years of scouting with the Reds, the three highest draft choices I had in the June draft were two second round picks in 1980 — Jim Pettibone rhp, Saguaro HS, Scottsdale, Arizona (from Houston as compensation for signing Joe Morgan as a free agent), and Kenny Jones, rhp, Arizona State — and a fourth round pick, Buddy Pryor, c, Arizona State, in 1982.

So most of the time I was scratching and clawing to try to find a decent ballplayer. Sometimes it happened, many times it didn't. It helps to be stoical if you're a baseball scout.

I was delighted to get Jerry Macias in the draft even though he was a low pick and an older player. He was a lefty who could throw strikes. I had a good feeling about him. Maybe, just maybe, this time he would be the one — the one to go all the way to The Show.

* * *

The Cincinnati Reds drafted Gerardo Macias in the twenty-fourth round of the 1981 June draft. He was a senior, left-handed pitcher from New Mexico State. I didn't see him pitch during the regular season, but I did get to see him at our annual tryout camp in Albuquerque just before the draft. At the tryout camp he threw 90 mph, but his curveball was too slow and he needed to come up with an effective change of pace.

Macias was 23 years old, had an excellent pitcher's physique (6-2, 185), was a fine athlete, a good citizen, a laudable student, married, and the father of a three-month-old son.

I called Les Houser, our scout in New Mexico, to tell him that we had gotten Macias in the draft and to make an appointment with Jerry so that we could sign him. We met late afternoon on the twelfth of June at the Howard Johnson in Las Cruces. I had flown to Albuquerque from Phoenix, and Les had picked me up at the airport and we had driven down to Las Cruces.

Jerry, who seemed overly nervous, was with his baseball coach, Jim Kwasny, who had been a friend of ours for years. There were also TV and radio people present, much to my surprise. Who tipped off the media about the signing? This never happens. You inform them *after* the player has signed.

Jerry and I had agreed at the tryout camp to a bonus of $1,000 if the Reds got him in the draft. Jerry wasn't a heavily scouted player; in fact, if we hadn't drafted him, he wouldn't have been drafted. He had said that he just wanted a chance to play, but he did express real concern about money because of his wife and son.

Jerry called me aside and said he wanted to talk to me. The general manager of the Chihuahua Dorados of the Mexican League had called the day before and made him an offer. I was shocked. I told Jerry I wasn't sure a Mexican team could legally negotiate with an American citizen who had been drafted. I had never heard of this happening.

I told Jerry our offer: $1,500 as a signing bonus, $600 a month, and the incentive bonus plan, which can be worth $7,500 to a player if he gets to the big leagues. The Mexican offer was $4,000 for the summer.

Jerry seemed resolved to sign with the Mexicans for these reasons: more money, he would be pitching in AAA, he could advance his career more quickly, he had played some amateur baseball in Chihuahua, and his wife wanted him to play in Mexico.

I called my boss, Joe Bowen, to explain this most unusual turn of events. He talked to Jerry, discussing the pros and cons of playing in Mexico. During the conversation Joe — a very shrewd man — asked Jerry how old he was. Jerry said he was 23 years old. At that instant Jerry's baseball stock crashed. A player starting out at 23 is an old player. I had suggested to Jerry at the tryout camp that maybe he should take a quick plunge in the fountain of youth and knock two years off his age. An organization simply can't stay as long with an older player as it can with a younger player.

After Jerry finished talking to Joe, I talked with Joe. We decided that the Reds should go through the Commissioner's Office to check on the legality of it all.

Everyone parted on friendly terms. Jerry was doing what he thought was in his best interest. I wished him good luck.

I didn't hear any more of the matter until the twentieth of June when Joe Bowen called me in Las Vegas where I was holding a tryout camp. The Commissioner's Office had informed the Reds that the signing of Gerardo Macias by Chihuahua was indeed illegal.

Immediately I put Houser on Jerry's trail. Houser immediately ran into difficulties. Jerry's parents, who lived in Phoenix, hadn't heard from him yet. Jerry and Linda Macias didn't have a telephone in their Las Cruces apartment. For that matter, Linda might not even be in Las Cruces, she might be with her family in Santa Fe, but we didn't have a name or number there. Coach Kwasny didn't know how to reach Jerry in Mexico. Houser used a Spanish-speaking girl from his All-State office in Albuquerque to track down Jerry in Chihuahua. She talked to numerous people before coming up with a hotel name.

I called the hotel. After talking to five people, I learned that Jerry had moved out of the hotel. I then called Bowen. The pressure from the Commissioner's Office to bring Macias back to the States was increasing. He said that I might have to go to Reynosa, Mexico, where Chihuahua would be playing soon.

I phoned the Reynosa Baseball Club to find out where the Chihuahua team would be staying, and at what time the game would start on Sunday.

I thought if I could talk to Jerry we could get everything settled quickly. We could meet in Las Cruces, I could sign him, and he could be on his way to Eugene, Oregon, to join our class A team there.

I finally reached Jerry at Hotel Amelia in Reynosa. I explained the situation to him. He was amazed. No one had told him anything. Not that he had been signed illegally, nor that the Chihuahua general manager had called the Reds asking permission for him to pitch out the season there.

I felt good after talking with Jerry, but I didn't feel that way after I talked to him the next morning. Jerry's manager was incensed because, as he told Jerry, the only reason we were interested in him was because Jerry was pitching in the Mexican League (knowledgeable baseball people rate the Mexican League the equivalent of a good American AA league), and that we were a cheap club for not bettering their offer. He also said that if we wanted Jerry, we would have to come down and get him.

The Mexican manager had struck a raw nerve with me when he called the Reds cheap. I had felt all along that we had to at least match the Mexican offer. It was a matter of face.

But a more pressing problem had arisen: how to get Jerry back to Chihuahua to pick up his belongings when he didn't have his tourist visa to get him back to Chihuahua in the first place. He had left his tourist visa in Chihuahua because it wasn't needed when he traveled with the team. There was an immigration station thirty miles from Reynosa, and without his tourist visa they wouldn't let him through.

To compound the problem, Jerry was to be paid $1,000 on the second of July when the team was in Monterrey.

I informed Bowen, who was in Billings, Montana, looking at our

Rookie team, of everything. He made it quite clear that I was to go to Mexico, get Macias out of there, sign him, and send him to Eugene. He had put his word on the line with the Commissioner's Office.

I called Jerry back and told him somehow, someway, we would get it all worked out. Neither one of us had a ready solution, but a plan evolved as we talked. I would fly to Brownsville, Texas, rent a car, drive the fifty miles to McAllen, cross the border in a cab and pick him up at Hotel Amelia, we would recross the border, spend the night in Brownsville, fly to El Paso the next morning, somehow get to Chihuahua, collect his belongings there, journey back to El Paso, sign him, and get him off to Eugene.

As we finished the conversation, I told him that five years from now we would both be able to laugh about this.

At 4:30 in the morning I was awakened by a phone call from Jerry. He said we had better meet at the baseball park and not at the hotel. He said there would be some "hassles" if we met at the hotel.

I arrived in Brownsville, rented a car, and headed for McAllen. I got to the International Bridge across from Reynosa around six in the evening. I negotiated with Jaime, a cab driver, for a round trip fare of $15. He wasn't supposed to be taking passengers across the border, so he drove down side streets to avoid the Mexican police.

As we drove on the half-paved, chuckholed, washboardy streets, great clouds of dust billowed up from the traffic. Jaime possessed a warm smile and an engaging sense of humor. At first I wondered if his cab would even go a block. There was a hole in the floorboard where my feet were supposed to go, and as we traveled over the streets, dust would spew up from the hole like an erupting volcano. When the car would shake as if in the throes of death, Jaime would laugh and say, "Great car. 50 cents more." When he would stop the car he would say, "Great brakes. 25 cents more."

When he would drive over a curb or nearly hit another car or a horse-drawn cart, I would say, "Bad driving. 50 cents off." And so it went all the way to the stadium.

As the cab pulled up to Estadio Adolfo Lopez Mateos, the Chihuahua team was walking through the entrance gates. I didn't see Jerry, so I asked a player on the team to go get him for me. Jerry came out of the dressing room. We both grinned as we shook hands. We spoke briefly and he went back in the dressing room to tell his coaches goodbye.

As I waited for Jerry, I talked to Roy Branch, a friendly, articulate black pitcher on the team, about playing baseball and living in Mexico.

Jerry came out and we left immediately. We rode with Jaime to Hotel Amelia where Jerry picked up his suitcase. We had no difficulty crossing the border.

As we drove to Brownsville we discussed how we were going to get to Chihuahua from El Paso. He still needed the tourist visa. He had gotten another player's tourist visa, but the other player was 30 years old and it said so on the visa.

We spent a short night in Brownsville, since we had to catch the 6:10 a.m. flight to Dallas. Jerry said he hadn't slept well. Neither had I.

The airplane took off and climbed into a surrealistic dawn scene: a horizontal layer of metallic gray clouds served as a floor for dancing white vertical clouds as an orange sun hung in a brilliant blue sky.

On the airplane Jerry talked about how his father had always said he was lucky. When he was born, his mother and father had entered him in a contest where the baby would be photographed free if his number were selected. It was. In high school in El Paso Jerry had signed up with the Air Force and only Jim Kwasny's persistence had gotten him out of that commitment. Kwasny offered Jerry a full baseball scholarship to New Mexico State, then convinced the Air Force recruiter that he was offering Jerry the better deal.

We flew on to El Paso from Dallas. We took a cab from the airport to the Mexican Consulate. Jerry told a woman bureaucrat that he had lost his tourist visa. I guess she had heard that story once too often. At least I got my tourist visa.

It was a long walk to the Aéromexico office carrying suitcases. Luckily, it was a cool day in El Paso, but unluckily, the airplane going to Chihuahua had already departed, so we had no other choice than to take the bus. We got directions to the bus depot and walked the two blocks.

Jerry tried to call Chihuahua's general manager while I bought the bus tickets. The general manager was in Guaymas, but his secretary hoped she could give Jerry his paycheck.

We boarded the bus and rode to Juarez where we changed buses. We were on the road using 1660 air conditioning: 16 windows down and 60 mph.

The highway out of Juarez was congested. It was dusty and smelled of diesel fumes. No one hesitated to pass on hills and corners. A truck very much out of alignment looked like an insect crawling on the highway. We hit a rainstorm farther on, but I could smell the sweet rain a mile before the drops fell. It cleaned and cooled the air.

Off in the distance I could see what could only be the immigration station. The moment of truth had arrived as the bus rolled to a slow stop. I was tense. Jerry showed some quick thinking just as the bus came to a stop. He had us change places so that I was sitting in the aisle seat. The immigration officials checked my papers very closely, for they needed to be stamped and I had to sign the copies. They didn't even look at Jerry's bogus tourist visa.

Some four hours later we arrived in Chihuahua. It was raining hard as Jerry and I stepped out of the taxi. There were only two rooms left at Hotel El Presidente. After Jerry inspected his room, he said, "This is the nicest, most expensive hotel I've ever stayed in.'

We were relaxed that night as we ate dinner at the hotel. The waiters recognized Jerry and asked him for his autograph.

The conversation and Bohemia beer flowed easily. Jerry talked about the ignorance of the Mexican peasants, how they could be bought off by the politicians, how they could never see the "big picture," and how education is the key to elevating your status in the world. He talked about the lack of opportunity for the people of Mexico, and about the people who go north for job opportunities. Some people send their families almost all the money they make, some send their families very little, and some never return.

I got up early and walked to Aéromexico's nearby office. All the seats were taken for the evening flight. So the choices were to fly stand-by, fly out the next morning, or take the bus.

I walked back to the plaza and had my shoes shined. Afterwards, I went inside the cathedral that dominates the plaza — the colonial architecture on the outside was more impressive than the interior, but it was cool and refreshing inside. I walked across the street to the hotel and met Jerry in the lobby. I gave him some pesos for cab fare. I went up to my room and filled out two contracts and the other required forms.

As I waited in the lobby I was getting worried. Jerry was two hours late. Finally he returned. He had gotten his paycheck and belongings. We hastily collected our things and took a cab to the bus depot. The bus depot was overcrowded, sweltering, and noisy. A madhouse. We got the last two seats on a bus that was just leaving for El Paso. Everything happened so fast that I hoped our suitcases had been loaded on the bus.

The speedometer wasn't working and there wasn't enough leg room, but there was air conditioning and taped music. The worst was over now. Would you believe a flat tire two hours later? Holy Chihuahua!

I got out of the bus to stretch my legs. A storm was rapidly moving in and the thunder sounded like approaching artillery, booming louder and louder. I was surprised that passengers helped the driver change the tire, and I was impressed that they weren't afraid to dirty their hands. It started to rain. Lightning struck close to the bus. I went back inside. Jerry was sleeping. It took them an hour to change the tire. The driver and his helpers boarded the bus drenched, with their soaked shirts clinging to their backs. I tried to sleep, but I was awakened by hail. The visibility was down to a hundred yards.

Suddenly, a gift from the heavens appeared. A fantastic sunset was created by an opening in the clouds. A yellow so vivid that I did not know such a color existed gushed from the opening. The contrast between this blazing yellow and the dark clouds was stunning. I stared at it until it faded from view.

Darkness quickly shrouded the land. I enjoyed the music from the tapes. I wished I were fluent in Spanish. But will we ever arrive in Juarez?

The windshield wipers were slowly mesmerizing me. I wished the bus driver would quit driving in the middle of the highway. We were going to make a dinner stop, but the town was blacked out. Good. Keep going.

At last the lights of Juarez shone through the rain-pelted windshield. The bus pulled into the bus depot. A light rain was falling as we got our suitcases, hailed a cab, drove across the border for the last time, and had the cab driver take us to three motels before we found rooms.

The next morning was a busy one. I had Jerry sign the contracts, we mailed them, we went to the bank, to the barbershop, to a sporting goods store to purchase a glove and baseball shoes, and finally to the airport.

It was nearly one o'clock and time for Jerry to board the airplane. We had been through a lot together. We shook hands, I wished him good luck, he thanked me for everything, I said some Spanish swear words he had taught me, we both laughed, and just before he disappeared into the airplane he turned and waved, and I waved back.

I turned around and walked to the gate where I would soon board an airplane for Phoenix.

*   *   *

Jerry didn't pitch well after reporting to Eugene. I visited him and Linda in Santa Fe in February. He was in a quandary over what to do, since he had just graduated in January, a job offer was pending, and Linda was pregnant again. She, however, wanted him to pursue his baseball dream. I learned later that Jerry Macias did not report to spring training.

*   *   *

Today Jerry is a field representative for New York Life. He and Linda live in Santa Fe with their three children. Jerry still plays baseball, pitching and playing first base or the outfield for a local semi-pro team.

NOTABLE QUOTES

"First, they had be be able to run like the devil because that's the only skill you use on both offense and defense. Then they had to be able to throw, and they had to have what Mr. Rickey called 'good body control.' We came up with tests to judge body control. Mr. Rickey believed a player could be taught to hit, and his theories have proved right."

— Rex Bowen
Scout, Cincinnati Reds

An autographed ball from Pete Rose to the author.
(ERIK HOWSAM)

8

Change of Pace

On the evening of May 27, 1974, I was at Phoenix Municipal Stadium watching a high school all-star game. Sitting next to me was my friend, John "Rocket" Miller, a part-time scout with the Houston Astros.

Rocket Miller had been a highly successful scout with Houston because he wasn't afraid to take chances. As we sat there watching the pre-game drills, two players in front of a dugout started to play burnout — throwing the ball as hard as they could to one another.

"Who's the tall kid?" asked Miller.

"He's the center fielder for Mesa High School," I said.

"What's his name?"

"Mickey Hatcher."

"Is he a prospect?"

"Not at this stage for me. He doesn't run well enough for the Reds."

"Humm. I like his make-up. I'm going to draft him."

"Because he's playing burnout?"

"Yeah."

I didn't believe him but a week later the June draft took place and sure enough I read in the newspaper that Mickey Hatcher had been drafted by the Houston Astros in the fourteenth round.

A day later I received a phone call from Rocket. I said, "Congratulations on getting Hatcher in the draft. Are you going to sign him?"

"I don't know. That's why I'm calling. When is your tryout camp in Phoenix?"

"Next week."

"Mind if I bring him out and run him in the 60?"

"No, not at all."

Rocket brought Hatcher out to East High School where I was holding the tryout camp. We ran Mickey in the 60-yard dash and he ran 7.2. Not terribly impressive.

Later Rocket told Hatcher that he thought he should go on to college. Mickey did go on to college where he excelled in both baseball and football, becoming an All-American junior college wide receiver at Mesa Community College. After Mesa, Hatcher went to Oklahoma where he again played both baseball and football. He signed with the L.A. Dodgers in 1977 after being selected in the fifth round.

I didn't come across Hatcher again until a few years later when I was scouting the Albuquerque Dukes, the Dodgers' AAA club in the Pacific Coast League. When I walked into the Albuquerque Sports Stadium before the game, there Mickey was, up in the stands in uniform talking with fans and signing autographs.

The rest is baseball history, fairy tale stuff. This player who is a throwback to the old days, who elevates the game by his zest and love for it, really of modest talent but who has a heart as big as the Grand Canyon, rises to star in 1988 in baseball's most hallowed moment, the World Series.

How strange life's twists and turns. . . . . . since I believe Mickey Hatcher is the only player ever to be drafted solely because he was playing burnout.

*   *   *

Early morning rays of sunlight bathe Waikiki. A man with a metal detector searches for coins and jewelry. A young man on a tractor drags the sand to smooth it out before waves of fleshy bodies descend upon the beach. Japanese tourists, snapping photographs, look like penguins lined up on a pier. Coconut palm trees sway gently in the trade winds. A jogger makes deep footprints in the wet sand. Old couples stroll along the beach. Two children are building a sand castle. A few people are swimming. A group of surfers farther out work the never-ending waves. Diamond Head juts up in the distance.

At night Waikiki transforms into a beach of flickering torches. Shadows from coconut palm tree tops make stars and starfish on the sand. Young lovers stroll along the beach. Live music emanates from hotels. Moored boats bob up and down in the water. Lighted boats, sailboats, ships, and freighters glide across the horizon. Overhead, airplanes with flashing lights prepare to land. Buoys with flashing red and blue lights mark the channel to the yacht marina. White chalk lines — the breaking surf — stretch and grow, and sometimes connect. The surf roars, stars shine, and a half moon hangs in the night sky.

But there's more to Hawaii than Waikiki. The islanders are nuts about sports. It's a place where West meets East on the playing fields. A place where sports from the West are played with the fanatical devotion of the East.

I have never seen so many joggers as I've seen in Honolulu. Hawaii's culture is the outdoors: sand, surf, sea, court, field, and baseball diamond.

Baseball fans look at the game differently in Hawaii. It's a chess match *extraordinaire* and each move is analyzed to the nth degree. What is missed by the average fan elsewhere isn't missed here. What's not appreciated elsewhere is appreciated in Hawaii.

The game is played with a different attitude as well. I can remember watching a game in the high school state tournament when the right fielder made a crucial error. Much to my surprise, the first baseman and shortstop sprinted out to console the right fielder.

There were other nice touches too. The umpires were decked out in aloha shirts. (Unfortunately, the wearing of aloha shirts didn't help the quality of the umpiring.)

Through the years I enjoyed watching the University of Hawaii play. They always had good players and competitive teams. Coach Les Murakami was treated like a wise man from the East by his assistant coaches. These hard-charging, butt-kicking, young lieutenants did most of the work, but the quiet, dignified, philosophical Murakami made the decisions.

Ironically, it was in this tropical paradise where I experienced my greatest disappointment in scouting.

I drafted Derek Tatsuno in the twelfth round of the 1976 June draft. Derek was a smallish (5-10, 150), left-handed pitcher from Aiea High School. I had seen Derek pitch the year before at old Honolulu Stadium during the state tournament. His senior year I saw him pitch twice during the state tournament at the new Aloha Stadium. The word was that Derek was too small to be a prospect.

But I didn't believe that. Derek showed me a nearly average major league fastball (we didn't have radar guns in those days), a good curveball, and the makings of a good straight change. He also had exceptional control of all his pitches. He was an outstanding competitor whose baseball intelligence was at the genius level. He rarely made a mistake on the baseball field. In addition, Derek was an excellent athlete: I saw him hit a home run over 400 feet, he could run, and he was the best fielding pitcher I have ever seen. If he had been bigger, he would have been a certain first round pick. I was delighted to get him in the draft.

I flew to Honolulu where I was met at the airport by Tony Sellitto, our scout in Hawaii, and the famed basketball coach at Maryknoll High School. We drove to Derek's home. Before we entered the house, we took off our shoes and left them outside on the porch. Derek had answered the door, his mother was in the kitchen, his grandfather was curled around a chair listening to a Japanese radio station with a portable radio, and his father — in a t-shirt and his undershorts — was watching television.

The TV was so loud that we couldn't talk. Mr. Tatsuno was so nervous that he could hardly function. I asked him if he wouldn't mind turning down the TV so that we could talk. The mother joined us in the discussion. We talked for a long time. Finally, I made them our offer and it was a fair offer for a twelfth round pick. (Today it would seem like peanuts.) I offered him a signing bonus of $12,500, plus the incentive bonus plan which would mean an extra $7,500 if he reached the major leagues. So a package deal of $20,000.

The Tatsunos wanted more time to evaluate the offer. I wanted to sign Derek, but I wasn't going to apply high-pressure salesmanship tactics. I hated it when someone did that to me. I told them that I would give them more time to talk it over, think about it, and arrive at a decision.

The one thing I would learn over the years was that it was difficult to get high school players off the islands. They weren't too anxious to leave paradise. I was shocked at the extensive, high-profile coverage that high school games and players received from the press. Outstanding high school athletes were treated like Hawaiian gods.

The next night I went to my first sumo wrestling match at Blaisdell Center. It was fascinating: the ritual, the costumes, the hairdos, the massive bodies, the struggle. I felt good that night. I was sure that Derek would sign.

When I called the next morning I was surprised to find out that Derek had decided not to sign. I tried to find out how much the father wanted, but he wouldn't tell me. It was a very long flight back to Arizona and, to rub salt into the wound, I had bought a Sunday newspaper to read on the airplane. When I came to the sports section, I read an account of our negotiations on the front page. I was enraged at this breach in confidentiality and good taste. I felt used in a cheap scheme to gain publicity.

Derek Tatsuno went on to have a brilliant career at the University of Hawaii. Unfortunately, by the time he was a junior and eligible for the draft again, his arm was worn out. He was never the same pitcher after this time. I saw him in the spring of 1979 at Cal-State Fullerton. There were more scouts at that game — 86 — than I had ever seen at one game. There were so many radar guns pointing at Tatsuno that I hoped he wouldn't be sterilized. Derek had a bad outing.

After that game, interest in Tatsuno dropped off sharply. I later heard that Derek was pitching in Japan. We didn't cross paths again until years later when I saw him pitch in Albuquerque for Hawaii in a Pacific Coast League game. He was just another breaking ball pitcher.

Derek Tatsuno is a legend in Hawaii. The people there haven't forgotten his sparkling performances in high school and college. But I will always believe that if Tatsuno had signed with the Reds out of high school, he would have had a fine major league career.

*   *   *

I met a modern-day David on June 16, 1985. The Goliath he slew was himself. David stood 3 feet 2 inches and weighed 128 pounds. He was a switch-hitting catcher.

Dave Stevens was participating in a tryout camp I was holding at Scottsdale Community College. Dave had no legs. He was a thalidomide baby from the late 1960s when women were taking that drug, a tranquilizer, during pregnancy.

I have never turned anyone away from a tryout camp, and I wasn't about to turn Dave away. He would be treated like all the other players. If anything, I knew that this special young man would make this a special day.

I always start a tryout camp by having the players run a 60- yard dash. When it was Dave's turn to run, everything else stopped. The silence was deafening. All eyes — parents, relatives, friends, college coaches, recommending scouts who were helping me, and the other 93 players — turned his way. Dave ran a 9 second 60.

I was amazed that he could scoot that fast on the palms of his hands. He gave *everything* he had in running that dash. Every cell, every fiber, every sinew, every muscle in his body strained to reach the finish line. Some people clapped, some cheered, some were stunned into silence, and some eyes grew moist.

I would let players try out at more than one position if they asked to, and Dave decided he wanted to throw with the outfielders. When it was his turn to make throws to second base, third base, and home plate, he became quite vociferous. I hit some ground balls to him with my fungo, but he started hollering at me to hit him some fly balls. Talk about pressure. It was like trying to drop a mortar round on top of him.

After the infielders threw, I timed the catchers throwing the ball down to second base. A pitcher throws the ball to the catcher, who is crouched behind home plate, and he throws out an imaginary runner trying to steal second. I would start the stopwatch the instant the ball hit the catcher's mitt and stop timing when the ball reached second base. A good time is 1.9

seconds. Dave was timed at 2.18 seconds. Quite respectable.

Now it was Dave's turn to hit. As one can imagine, it was difficult to find a pitcher who could throw a strike to Dave's small strike zone. Dave made some contact with the bat. He did, however, have trouble hitting against a left-handed pitcher. He had never seen one in high school.

After he hit, I let him put on the mask and chest protector and go behind the plate. I wish that every catcher would take charge behind the plate like Dave did.

The tryout camp ended. Dave was being interviewed by a newspaper reporter, then by a TV sportscaster. I got to talk to him before he left. I told him that I thought he had a great career ahead in coaching because he would be such an inspiration to his players. Dave talked about getting into sports broadcasting on either radio or TV. I told him that whatever he chose to do in life, he would be a success. No man with that type of fierce determination could end up a failure.

That summer day in June, Dave Stevens stood as tall as any man. Indeed, he was a giant among men. No one ever gave more of himself at a tryout camp than Dave gave at mine. The last thing he told me was, "If you don't have dreams, you don't have anything."

*   *   *

Today Dave Stevens is a television sports producer in Minneapolis.

NOTABLE QUOTES

Larry Barton, Jr. and I were having a relaxed conversation with Kenny Jones after signing him to a contract. Jones, a fine-looking Arizona State pitcher, said he was getting married the second. Somewhat surprised, I said, *"The second?"*

"Yeah, the second it becomes absolutely necessary."

*"You can't pitch like that. If you're going to walk them, then walk them with **authority**."*

—Thornton Lee
at a spring training game

Thornton "Lefty" Lee
(EDWIN HOWSAM COLLECTION)

9

Lefty

My most unforgettable character in baseball is a man nearly forty years my senior. His name is Thornton "Lefty" Lee.

I first met Lefty when I came to Arizona in 1971. He was a part-time scout with the St. Louis Cardinals. Lefty became my mentor, my confidant, my grandfather. We picked grapes and made raisins together; we cut firewood together; and we fished for bass and hunted quail together.

Lefty had a nimble mind. He was curious about everything. He always had a book that he was reading by his chair. He had an incredible memory, a splendid sense of humor, and was a gifted storyteller. Many of his baseball stories were spellbinding, and often times hilarious. But Lefty was also a horse of a man — the strongest man at 70 I've ever seen.

When traveling with Lefty you received a running commentary about everything. His knowledge of Arizona history, mining, geology, flora, and fauna was staggering.

Lefty had had quite a baseball career. He was an all-star pitcher — he pitched in the 1941 All-Star Game for the American League. He pitched 16 years in the big leagues, mostly with the Chicago White Sox.

In 1941 — his best year — he was 22 and 11, led the league with an ERA of 2.37, pitched 300 innings, and started 35 games and completed a league-leading (and mind-blowing) 30 games.

As a scout Lefty had the remarkable ability of being able to analyze a pitcher almost instantly. It was astonishing what he could tell you about a pitcher after watching him only for a minute.

*   *   *

"I was born in Sonoma, California. The home of Jack London. Jack London and *I* both come from Sonoma. (He laughs.) My father was working in the orchards. They raised a tremendous amount of apples, prunes, and pears around there, and he was helping and supervising the planting of these orchards.

"My mother and my oldest sister had asthma, so we were continually trying to get away from the coast to alleviate their condition, and we would go farther south. We moved quite a bit when I was a youngster. We even came down to Willcox, Arizona, hoping it would be the answer. But my parents couldn't take the heat in the summertime, plus we were 65 miles from the nearest doctor and schools, so when us kids got ready to go back to school, we moved to California around Arroyo Grande. That's where I went to high school, and started in playing baseball. In fact, I played all sports: football, basketball, baseball, and track. When I graduated from high school I was 6-3, 195, which was pretty big in those days. Then I went on to Cal Poly.

"I went up to Paso Robles over Easter break and worked out with the Pittsburgh Pirates in 1925. But I didn't sign with them because my dad said that they were a bunch of bums. I got summer jobs in the oil fields over in Taft, California, and pitched over there because I could make good wages and $75 a ball game, pitching twice a week.

"They didn't have scouts in those days but Danny W. Long, a friend of Charlie Comiskey, and a police magistrate in San Francisco, happened to be on vacation and came out and saw me pitch against San Jose State Teachers College in San Luis Obispo and I had a pretty good game. Typically, I struck out a lot of them and walked a lot of them — actually I set a record for strikeouts with 18 that wasn't broken until 1950. Danny wrote Comiskey, the owner of the White Sox, and I still have the contract today where he offered me $350 a month, and Pullman transportation to and from my home to Chicago. Quite a little difference between that $350 and nowadays. Now they have more strings of goose eggs! I didn't sign with the White Sox because my father insisted that I finish my education.

"In the spring of 1927 the San Francisco Seals sent a man down on the recommendation of one of the old-time ballplayers, Dan Sheehy, who was an infielder with Portland. I went up and signed with them for spring training, but they had a tremendous pitching staff left over from the year before — 11 regulars. Among the rookies trying to make the club were Lefty Gomez, Curt Davis, and myself. Eight out of the twelve rookies that came into camp eventually went to the big leagues. The Seals got me a semi-pro job in California up in the logging camps. I worked for the Diamond Match Company in Susanville and Stirling City. It was there that I got my leg crushed in a logging accident. That's what slowed me down getting to the big leagues. I spent five months in the hospital with a compound fracture, then infection set in. After the accident I wore an aluminum shin guard with a felt liner all my career.

"I got a job down in the oil fields in late October and I pitched in the winter league. I knew some of the managers. In those days some of the Coast League ballplayers played in the winter league. Guys like Buzz Arlett, Del Baker, Jack Fenton, Rusty Firebaugh. They all kept working on their jobs, but they kept playing all year around.

"The next year San Francisco signed me again and sent me, Dolf Camilli, Lefty Gomez, and a whole bunch of us to Salt Lake City in the Utah-Idaho League. I got into a beef with the manager, Bobby Coltrin, because he wanted me to pitch overhand and I had to pitch 3/4. So I was released.

"After I was released I pitched semi-pro ball in Price, Utah. That following winter I played in the winter league again.

"The San Francisco Seals tried to sign me again in 1929, but an old-time pitcher, Mickey Shader, had gotten the Globe club in the Arizona State League. He signed me for $250 a month, and the copper company paid me another $100. Well, the Seals were offering me a contract for $250 a month. Flat. You know where I went.

"We only played five games a week. We were off two days. That enabled us to get up to the mine to punch the time clock. We traveled in one of those old-time Cadillac buses with five seats in it; a touring car, cloth top, dirt roads, no air conditioning, your luggage strapped on the left side, and away you went.

"We had breakdowns all the time. Flat tires. You name it. We took rifles with us and if there weren't any hawks or insulators to shoot at, we would make a target out of folded paper, all pitch quarters in a cap, set the target out there, and see who would get the jackpot.

"I beat neighboring Miami six times that year. Lots of rivalry between the two little towns. Tony Freitas and I pitched a doubleheader against Miami on the fourth of July. We beat them a doubleheader. That night as we were going down to the local restaurant to eat dinner, the miners, gamblers, and all were peeling off bills. Not very big ones but we took in quite a bit of money on the way down to eat.

"Tony Freitas and I pitched a doubleheader in August in Phoenix and both games went 13 innings. The temperature that day was 118°. Well, now, that's quite a chore. But I'll tell you the thing that stands out in my mind today. Buck Woodson, the catcher we had — we only had 15 players on the squad — Buck Woodson played second base the first game, and caught the second game.

*   *   *

"I met my wife, Esther, while I was playing ball for Globe. She was a Miami girl. We got married in December, 1929. That's what caused the Crash and the Depression!

"That fall in the draft I was one of the few ballplayers who was drafted by a Class B ball club from a Class D ball club. There was an umpire in the league by the name of George Blackburn, an old, heavy-set fellow from Tyler, Texas. He recommended me to Pop Kitchens, who was managing Tampa in the Southeastern League.

"In 1930 I went down to Tampa and all during spring training Pop Kitchens was trying to peddle me to the Detroit Tigers or the Brooklyn Dodgers because he had a 25% clause in his contract.

"I got off to a bad start there. I won 3 and lost 9. Then I got started. I found out what I was doing on my stride and I changed my stride. I threw a one-hitter and struck out 17 in Columbus, Georgia. Then we went to Montgomery, Alabama, and the scouts were there. I went out one Sunday and pitched a no-hitter and struck out 15. Then we went over to Pensacola, Florida, and I struck out 19 and pitched a two-hitter. I won six in a row and they sold me to Cleveland. I finished the season with New Orleans. Memphis beat us out for the pennant.

"I spent spring training with Cleveland and New Orleans. But they had seven left-handed pitchers in New Orleans and they only had one in Shreveport. Jakey Atz of Shreveport wanted a left-hander, so he sent Vern Underhill over to New Orleans, and New Orleans sent me over to Shreveport.

"Shreveport had lost their first 12 ball games. The day that I reported they got beat in Wichita Falls, and Jakey come hobbling into the clubhouse, took off his cap and put it up in his locker, turned to the players, and said, 'Well, champs, you can't win 'em all.'

"You are not going to believe this, but we went 67 innings without scoring a run. I know because I got beat 1-0 in 11 innings in Wichita Falls by Ash Hillen. Then we went over to Dallas four days later and I pitched against George 'Tar Heel' Murray and he beat me 1-0 in 13 innings. Then we went down to Galveston and 'Black Bill' Harris, who later pitched with the Pirates, beat me 1-0 in 10 innings. We couldn't score runs with pencils.

"I'll give you a sideline on Jakey. He started his career way back around the turn of the century and he had the name of Zimmerman, and they paid off alphabetically and when they got to Z they didn't have any money left in the treasury. So the next year when he came to spring training, they said, 'Zimmerman are you ready to sign?' He said, 'The name isn't Zimmerman. It's Atz. A-t-z. I'm sure as hell going to get paid this year.'

"He was quite a character. He'd have a meeting. We were playing all night ball then because attendance was down. It was during the Depression and you couldn't get very many people into the ballpark. But Jakey would have a meeting at ten in the morning. He would tell us who was going to pitch and catch that night, and then he'd reach in his back pocket and pull out a racing form and say, 'So-and-so looks good in the 5th race at Arlington today.'

"Another time the guys were drinking quite a bit of home brew. One of the groundskeepers had a little place behind the stands where they made the home brew and sold it. After the ball game at night he'd have all the lights blacked out on the outside but lighted on the inside and he'd sell home brew. Jakey told us one day — we were having a meeting — 'Now the story has come to me that some of you fellas are drinking too much beer. I want you to know that I'm not going to mention any names, but Tuero and Moulton, you be careful.'

"I remember one occasion in Beaumont. Jakey came storming into the coffee shop at the hotel one morning, walked by all the players, and then back out again. Well, that afternoon before the ball game we had another meeting. He said, 'Fellas, the name is Atz. A-t-z. Not Astor. Go easy on those meal checks.'

"Jakey was getting along in years. He had managed and won so many games and so many titles when he was with Fort Worth, but that was the kind of fellow he was. He was one of the most colorful characters in baseball.

"Joe Engel, the owner of Chattanooga, was another character. He had a shortstop named Johnny Jones. In fact, I pitched against Jones. In one game in New Orleans he sawed off about two inches of his bat right there in the dugout and said, 'I'm going to get around on you next time.' And he's sawing it off. Johnny Jones. Anyway, he had a clause in his contract that if he was sold he would get a percentage of the purchasing price. Joe Engel sold him for a turkey and invited him to the banquet so he could get his percentage of the purchasing price. That was Joe Engel.

*   *   *

"I told you about the night games. There was an oddity — you know who pitched one of the first night games down there in the Southern League? It was Leo Moon. Moon pitched a night ball game.

"They had the big, old, giant lights that had three big bulbs and reflectors and every time it rained, they would start popping like pop corn all over the place. We had an amusing thing happen in the American Association years later. Joe Oliveras, a Cuban infielder, was hitting one night and I was pitching in Louisville. Monte Pearson came out and relieved me, thunderstorm coming up, lights are popping and flashing, going out and it's getting darker, and Pearson is throwing BBs up there and Joe Oliveras backed out of the box. The umpire said, 'What's the matter, Joe, don't you want to hit?' Joe gave the bat to the umpire and said, 'You take it.'

"Roxie Lawson told me he was in the Three-I League, and Earl Wolgamot was managing the club. They were battling the Detroit farm club for the pennant, and Tommy Bridges was the pitcher, as a kid. The count went to 3-2 and Lawson looked down to third base for the sign, and Wolgamot gave him the take sign. Here comes a fastball right down the middle and he took it and was called out. He got in the clubhouse and walked over to Wolgamot and said, "Wolgie, what in the world did you give me the take for?' Wolgie said, 'You're a better hitter taking than you are swinging.'

"There were a number of characters in the minors at that time. 'Raw Meat' Rodgers, Spencer Abbott, and John King just to name a few. 'Raw Meat' actually ate raw meat. He'd put a little salt on it and then eat it. Of course, he always drank enough so he killed all the bugs in the raw meat! Spencer Abbott. He was in the Coast League. He ribbed all the ballplayers all the time on both clubs. He was coaching third base one night and Bill Dietrick hit a triple — it was a double but he tried to stretch it into a triple — and the ball and all of them came together at third base, the umpire, Dietrick sliding in, and here comes Abbott from the coaching box sliding in from the other side. Yeah, Spencer Abbott.

"John King, who later became a multimillionaire in the oil fields and an umpire in the Texas League, was quite a character. He *hated* left-handed pitchers. If he saw anybody left-handed that was it. He wouldn't talk, shake hands, or anything else. They tell the story about him going down the sidewalk one day, and there was a guy sitting there with a cap in his hand. John reached in his pocket and got a quarter and dropped it in the cap. The old fellow said, 'Bless you.' John started on down the street and he looked back and the old guy had a violin and grabbed the bow and started playing left-handed. John walked back and reached down and got his quarter and took it out of the cap and went down the street. John King.

"He was a left-handed hitter and he couldn't hit left-handed pitchers worth a darn, but he could chew up the right-handers. They ran him out one night after he had hit a home run earlier in the ball game. He walked out to the outfield fence and got the 1 off the scoreboard and took it into the clubhouse and said, 'If I can't play, then you can't have my run.'

"There was an umpire named Steamboat Johnson, mostly in the Southern League, who also was a real character. He was one of the funniest guys you ever saw in your life. An argument would break out at the plate over balls and strikes — at that time they could protest them — and they would run up and he would argue with them for a moment, then he'd reach in his pocket and pull out an Ingersol watch and say, 'I'll give you two minutes to clear the field.' And there were no hands on the watch.

"On a called third strike, he wouldn't call a man out or call a third strike, he would spiral his finger over his head and say, 'And he knew it!' When he was umpiring down at first base and a ground ball was hit to the infield, he would say to the hitter running down the line, 'Turn to your right.'

*   *   *

"I played under Walter Johnson in Cleveland. Old Walter was a great gentleman, a grand fellow, but he was not a manager. He expected all the pitchers to be like him. Of course, there was only one Walter Johnson and he would second-guess you on every pitch and that's the worst thing in the world. You would throw a curveball and someone would click it. You'd go back to the bench and he would say, 'What did he hit?' You'd say, 'Curveball.' He never swore in his life — Walter was very religious and a very clean living guy — so he would say, 'Good, gosh almighty, you know he was looking for a curve. Come in here with that fastball. In on him. Crowd him.' Walter could do it consistently, but there weren't too many Walter Johnsons around. Hornsby was the same way. Everything came so easily to them that they expected everyone to go out and duplicate it. That's one of the tough situations.

"I saw Walter Johnson pitch in an exhibition game against Michigan State at East Lansing. I think it was in 1934. An oddity of the thing was that the leadoff man for Michigan State knocked the cap right off his head with a line drive on the first pitch of the game.

"One time we were on a losing streak. We hadn't been scoring any runs. Finally, Walter came out and said that he was going to throw batting practice, just to the left-handed hitters. He said that anybody who hits that right field wall, which was very short in Cleveland at 290 feet, gets a bonus. He went out there and threw 20 minutes and nobody hit that wall. He was 46 years old. Walter was a low 3/4 pitcher and that's why he never had the good curveball. It was more of a slider than it was a curveball. It didn't have the good rotation to break the ball down.

"Johnson had a tremendous fastball and tremendous movement on it. Patsy Gharrity, the coach, told us that he was hitting against Johnson onetime and he choked up to get around on him and hit the ball on the part of the bat that was choked up.

"He threw over 100 mph. Johnson's the only one that Feller asked if he thought he was as fast as he was. Johnson said, 'Yes, I believe I was faster than you are.' All the baseball writers at that time agreed that Johnson was faster than Feller.

"I had a bad arm in the spring of 1934 and they used me in nothing but relief. The only time I pitched was when someone else didn't want to pitch against the Yankees or Washington. We were in New York one day and Walter Johnson came in and had a new ball and he walked over to Pearson and said, 'Do you want to pitch today?' Monte was his fair-haired boy. He said, 'Walter, I would like to have a couple of more days of rest. My shoulder is a little stiff.' And he stretched his arm. Walter said okay and turned around. He then walked over to Hildebrand. Now Hildebrand was a very sarcastic individual. Just the way he would say 'Good morning,' you'd want to punch him right in the nose. I know because I roomed with him. Walter walked over to Hildebrand and told him that he was pitching. Hildebrand said, 'Well, if Monte can get two more days with four days rest, I ought to be able to get two with two days rest.' Unbeknownst to Walter, Hildebrand was Billy Evans' fair-haired boy, the general manager's fair-haired boy. Johnson said, 'Any time you've got that uniform on, you've got to be ready to pitch. I pitched three shutouts on three consecutive dates in this town in 1908.' Hildebrand said, 'Yeah, and baseball was quite a bit different then.' Walter said, 'Oh, a wise guy.' And Hildebrand said, 'I may not be too wise, but I'll answer any question you can think of.' Johnson whirled and said, 'That's a hundred dollars and go take your uniform off.' Hildebrand said, 'I'll go take my uniform off, but it's not going to cost me a hundred dollars.' Johnson turned to me and said, 'You're pitching.' I said, 'Yes, sir.' Boy, I didn't give him any argument. They weren't going to take anything I was making. We went out and scored 8 runs in the first inning and we beat Red Ruffing 12-3. When we were in the showers, Pearson came by me and said, 'Gee, if I'd known we was going to get that many runs, I would have pitched it myself.' I said, 'Thanks a lot.'

"When we went back home, Walter Johnson was still fuming and it was sticking in his craw the way Hildebrand had shown him up in front of all the ballplayers talking the way he did. When we went back home, Oral Hildebrand went right upstairs to Billy Evans and stated his case and it never cost him any money. Well, you're not going to have discipline with two factions on a club. Incidentally, when the season was over, Hildebrand was the ringleader in taking up a collection to present Billy Evans a Rolex watch. One of the guys told Hildebrand to give Evans the hundred dollars he had saved him.

*   *   *

"I saw Bobby Feller win his first ball game. He was a 17-year-old farm boy. It was an exhibition game against the Cardinals. Steve O'Neil went out to catch him. He put the stuff on and went behind the plate. The first pitch was slightly to the right and Steve went over with the glove to catch it and it hit the screen behind him. Steve just took off the gear and called Greek George out. The Greek was back there with his right hand behind him and he had an old catcher's mitt that was all beat up and he's back there snapping at them when they're going by. The kid struck out 7 out of 9. Bobby would give you the big windup, look at third base, throw home, and then turn to see where the ball went.

"His first pitch in his first American League game made him. Do you remember Lyn Lary with the rubber legs, dancing around up at the plate, going through all those gyrations? Feller wound up with that first pitch, looked the third base coach in the eye, turned it loose, and looked to see where it went. He just burnt all the hair off the back of Lyn Lary's neck. I mean it. It didn't miss him by that much. Lary got up — he took 4 Ks that day — but that front foot was going for the dugout every time Bobby wound up. Boy, could he fire! The next time out, Feller had 17 strikeouts against the Athletics.

"Feller had a blazing fastball and a real good curveball, better than a lot of people thought. His curveball would get that part of the plate but it was so quick and so fast and so big, the umpires missed a lot of curveballs on him. I believe he threw 12 one-hitters in his career. Boob McNair said it best about Feller. When he was asked what it was like to hit against Feller, he said, 'It was like somebody flipping aspirin tablets at you right at sundown and you try to hit them with baling wire.'

*   *   *

"The Chicago White Sox got me in a three-cornered trade in 1937. I went to Washington, and Washington traded me to Chicago for Jack Salveson.

"I had the pleasure of working with two outstanding baseball men in Chicago, Muddy Ruel, the pitching coach, and Jimmy Dykes, the manager.

"Muddy was a great pitching coach. Muddy would never answer a question you asked him. He would ask you a question and make you answer your own question and that way you remembered it.

"Jimmy Dykes was the best manager I ever played for. He was a great manager for the material that he had and the amount of money he had to operate with. And he used about as good as strategy with what he had as anybody I ever saw. Jimmy made each ballplayer feel that he was really deserving. He was the kind of guy who went along with you 100% and never second-guessed you. Not a whole lot of backslapping, not a rah-rah guy, just firm, quiet support. He gave you confidence by telling you that you could do it.

"I'll give you an insight on Dykes. My first start for the White Sox was against Washington and I went out there and they scored four runs off me in the first inning. Dykes goes out there and says, 'I'm going to take you out, but you're the next hitter. Go on home and forget about it.' I walked up to the plate and hit one off Monte Weaver in the upper deck in Chicago and came into the dugout and grabbed my glove and jacket. Dykes said, 'Hey, wait a minute. I might want to put you in at first base.' I looked at him and said, 'Well, if you need the power.' And he said, 'Go on. Get out of here.' Five days later the Yankees came into town and he told me that I was the pitcher. I won the game.

*   *   *

"I had a very good sinker. I could throw it from high 3/4 or low 3/4. I didn't grip the seams of the ball, I just let it slip out. It was tougher to control, but it was very heavy and it didn't have rotation on it, so it would sink.

"When I wanted to mark up the ball, I wouldn't do it myself. I'd have the first baseman do it for me. Kuhel had loose eyelets in the webbing of his glove. He'd catch the ball up in there and turn it and the eyelets would cut the ball. My luck was always that the hitter would foul it off on the first pitch into the stands.

"I would only do this when a new ball came out, and if there was a man on. I'd make a couple of throws over to first base. Generally, the second time he'd catch the ball and start towards the mound, so I knew when the ball had been doctored. But I hardly ever did this. I didn't need to. I had a good sinker. It was heavy, real heavy. Guys hated to warm me up.

*   *   *

"I believe the best one I ever saw for sheer speed was Lefty Grove. I honestly believe he was faster than Feller. When he would throw his good, hard one — the ball would get about six feet from the plate and then you just lost it. Tremendous. You'd think about swinging and the glove was popping behind you already. I hit one foul ball into the third base dugout and put it down as a base hit off of him.

"Grove was a surly, mean competitor. And I mean he was a

competitor. If you tried to drag bunt off of him, he would rear back and bore you right in the middle of the back on the next pitch if the ball went foul. He wouldn't cover first base. He would stand on the rubber and watch the play.

"Dykes told the story about Grove when the rivalry between New York and Philadelphia was ferocious, and the New York papers came out with the story that no wonder Grove was having such a great year in 1931 — he won 31 games that year — he never wanted to pitch against the Yankees. Grove had pitched two days before. Connie Mack was having a meeting and the clubhouse door opened up and in came Grove. He walked right over and took the ball right out of Connie Mack's hand and said, 'Give me this.' He walked out, started the ball game, and he had to quit in the 5th inning with blood blisters on his fingers, and he had struck out 12 in 5 innings.

"He had such an easy, flowing delivery and he had such great wrists that he would pop them. He threw over the top. He relied on his fastball. It wasn't until years later when he got to Boston that he developed a good curveball.

"One time Al Simmons hit me. I was pitching in League Park against Philadelphia — I told you about my shin guard — and Simmons hits a screamer. Wham! Bam! Hit the shin, bounced up in the air, came down, I stood there and caught it, and I threw him out at first base. Simmons wasn't a gazelle, and he was going down the first base line hollering and cussing me.

"Well, they went from Cleveland down to Washington. Then we go on the road and follow them. We get down to Washington. Bump Hadley is pitching for Washington against us and I'm hitting. He's got two strikes on me, and I had just hit one ball foul out of the ballpark. He came back with his good curveball and hit me right on the front of that shin. I flipped the bat away and trotted down to first base. Joe Kuhel, Washington's first baseman, says, 'Aren't you going to rub? That hit you right smack on the shin.' And I said, 'He ain't got enough to make anybody rub.' He looked at me kind of funny and didn't say anything. Years later we traded for Kuhel and when he came into spring training I was putting on my uniform and when he saw me lacing on the shin guard, he said, 'Oh, now I know why you're so big and rough and tough. You know a funny thing about that. Just a couple of days before you guys came in, Simmons told me that he raked that Lee off the hill, you didn't rub, threw him out, and finished the ball game. Simmons said he thought he had hit the ball pretty hard. Then you come down there, Hadley hits you solid, and you didn't rub.'

"I used to throw changes inside to Joe DiMaggio to get ahead of him. I felt sorry for the fans sitting down the third base line because he would hit those screaming line drives into the stands. Then I would try to get him to go for the pitch down and away. Unfortunately, I didn't have much luck with DiMaggio. He gave me lots of trouble.

"But the best right-handed hitter I ever faced was Rogers Hornsby. I faced him in an exhibition game in 1930 in Tampa. The thing I never forgot was his complete confidence at the plate.

"In those days they knocked you down and you expected it. I can recall one of the stories about Charlie Grimm when they started a dusting bee. It was getting hotter all the time and Charlie walked to the plate to hit — he was a left-handed hitter — and he turned to the umpire and called time and lay down on the ground and yelled, 'All right, go ahead and pitch.'

"Ted Williams was the best left-handed hitter I ever faced. He was such a great hitter that they tried to pitch too carefully to him. Nibblers. Then they would get behind in the count, have to throw the fastball over the plate, and it was Katie-bar-the-door. He'd jump on the cripple.

"A funny story involved my son, Don, and Ted Williams. Don had just given up a home run to Ted in Boston, and Ted was really giving it to him going around the bases. Ted was saying, 'Take that you S.O.B. One off your old man, one off you. Now it's time to quit.'

"The good hitter may decoy you the first time up. Joe Kuhel used to do that. He'd come up with no one on. The pitcher would make a good pitch with a fastball down and in. Kuhel would jump back and argue with the umpire, but he was decoying the pitcher all the time. Late in the ball game he would come up with men in scoring position, and he knew he was going to get that same pitch because he had jumped back and taken it. He'd wind up with the pitcher and knock it out of the park.

"Bing Miller told this story on himself. He went to spring training and the pitchers weren't sharp in spring training with their breaking stuff, so he kept looking for the breaking pitches and he'd climb on those all the time. He started the rumor that he could hit the curveball with anybody. Consequently, when the season started he got nothing but fastballs to hit. If it was a curveball he'd just take it. They never did throw him a lot of curveballs.

"I pitched against Babe Ruth a couple of times in 1933. I hit him on the uniform roll near the knee with a slow sidearm curveball with two strikes on him. He hobbled around, clenched his fist, found a soft spot, and laid down on the ground. The papers blasted me. There was a picture of me in the throwing motion. This was during the time when John Dillinger, the gangster, was raising heck in the Midwest and the caption read: 'Why keep the good burghers and the militia awake all night trying to catch Dillinger? Why not let Lefty take a pot shot at him?'

"Another time Ruth hit into a double play. Hale was playing second base and playing back so deep on the grass in right field that he was shaking hands with Dick Porter, the right fielder. Hale had to catch the ball or it would have gone right through him. They doubled up Ruth before he got away from the plate. He was three steps down the line hollering, 'Get in the ballpark!'

"Lou Gehrig was a great left-handed hitter. Lots of power. A good high ball hitter. He had a very strong, short, quick stroke. When I was first up there, he was a left field hitter. He hit most of his home runs to left field and left center. Later on he pulled everything to the right of second base. Gehrig was a great guy. Quiet. Never said anything to anybody.

"Charlie Gehringer was the same way. He would say two words a year, so we nicknamed him 'Rowdy.' Lefty Gomez said that you could put Curt Davis and Charlie Gehringer in the same room and walk in any time day or night and hear the clock ticking.

"Gehringer never made an error. We also called him 'The Robot' or 'The Mechanical Man.' He always got a base hit. He was the greatest *picture* left-handed hitter I ever saw.

"Getting back to Ruth. Ruth was more dramatic than Gehrig. Gehrig was a workman who got the job done. Ruth right at the dramatic moment of the ball game would come through, and he seemed to always come through in the big games. Ruth was, of course, when I saw him getting heavy, older, but he was still a great ballplayer as far as defense and everything. He could throw with pretty near anybody, and he was accurate with his throwing.

"I think he was the all-time, greatest ballplayer. He was a great pitcher, one of the best. He did more for baseball than anybody else. It was at a crucial time after the scandal. Baseball was suffering in attendance until he started bashing balls out of the ballpark.

"I played with two pretty fair ballplayers at Chicago, Ted Lyons and Luke Appling. Ted was a great athlete. A great competitor. A great fielder. A great fellow. When he was young he was really quick. In later years he used a slow curveball with a knuckleball. He was very popular with the fans. You win a lot of ball games for a last place, or perpetually second division club, you've got to be some kind of pitcher.

"Luke Appling was one of the greatest hitters to fight off the pitch to get what he wanted to hit, which was generally the curveball. He was one right-handed hitter who could hit Feller's curveball good. One year Bob Kennedy kept count — Bob wasn't playing regularly then, I think it was his first year up — and Appling hit over 700 foul balls into the stands over the course of the season.

"The worst hitter I ever saw was a pitcher by the name of Howard Craghead. In old Recreation Park in San Francisco it was 265 feet down the right field line. Craghead had gone over 100 at bats without a base hit. He hit a line drive to right field and when he saw it go over the second baseman's head, he turned to the dugout and give 'em the old clenched fist and started running to first base. Smead Jolley, the right fielder, who had one of the best arms I ever saw, threw Craghead out at first base.

"Mike Tresh came out to me one day. A thunderstorm was approaching. It was still and quiet and hot and humid as hell. He said, 'For Christ's sake, the beer's getting hot, let's get out of here.' He turned around and walked back to home plate. Now that's *serious* strategy.

"Ted Lyons nicknamed Jimmy Fox 'The Beast.' Fox hit two home runs in Chicago over the left field *roof*. Lefty Gomez said when he first went to wearing glasses, he got up on the mound, looked in there, and there was Fox, standing there with that bat, flexing his muscles. Gomez said that he took off his glasses and put them into his pocket because he didn't want those muscles breathing at him.

"Dizzy Dean had the great control, the great curveball, and he threw hard. He was mean along with it. He'd see a hitter digging a hole and he'd say, 'Dig it deep enough because that's where I'm going to bury you.' He was a good hitter and a good baserunner. He could wheel-and-deal. Diz had a sweeping motion — real fluid.

"Carl Hubbell told me that he tried to throw all his pitches out of the same motion. He didn't throw too hard. He was just an ordinary pitcher until he came up with that screwball — and he had more than one type of screwball. He had one that broke straight down, and another one that drifted. Carl was the best money pitcher I ever saw. He beat Dizzy Dean in one of the greatest pitching feats when he beat Diz 1-0 in 18 innings and didn't walk a man.

"Hack Wilson did a lot of nightclubbing and a lot of drinking. He'd get plastered every night when they were home, so Joe McCarthy, the Cubs' manager, would come walking through the clubhouse and here would be Hack with his head inside the locker and his feet in there and he'd be putting on his sanitary hose and McCarthy would have a cigar in his mouth, unlit, and McCarthy would tap him on the shoulder and say, 'Give me a match, will you.' Hack would reach in and get a book of matches and hand them to him and go right on dressing because he didn't want to face around where McCarthy could smell the fumes. McCarthy would go into his office and read what was on the match book. What tavern it was and so forth. After batting practice he'd call Hack into the office and say, 'Now we know you were out last night at such-and-such a place.' Hack would come out on the field ready to play and say, 'That guy's got spies everywhere. He's got detectives watching me.' Hack never did find out where McCarthy was getting all the information. Giving it to him from his own book of matches!

*   *   *

"Who was my best sign? Oh, it had to be John Denny. He was out of Prescott, Arizona. The Cardinals took him in the twenty-ninth round in 1970. We gave him $500 to sign. Later he won the Cy Young Award in 1983.

"I remember talking to John after he signed — and that leads to your next question — and he asked me what advice I would give him about pitching. I told him to keep the ball down, get it over the plate, stay ahead of the hitters, and develop a good change. I understand he came up with one of the best changes in the business.

"When I scouted a pitcher I first looked at the physical aspects: size, arm, and delivery. The last thing I looked at was control. You know that will eventually come. Also, you know he's going to get a little faster playing and working out every day, and get a little tougher as he grows up and matures. Then you consider stamina and desire. But first you have to have the physical ability.

"I wouldn't trade my baseball experiences for anything. It was a great life. The players enjoyed the game more then than they do now. They talked baseball, they ate baseball, and they lived baseball. Now they're too busy counting their money."

*   *   *

Lefty lives in Tucson. This all-star of a man celebrated his 88th birthday on September 13, 1994.

Action at a tournament in Taipei, Taiwan.
(EDWIN HOWSAM)

10

The Chinese Connection

It was raining as the plane landed in Tokyo. The blue runway lights cast an eerie glow in the brownish-gray ground fog.

Seas of people surged through the chaotic terminal. I hadn't slept on the nearly eleven-hour flight from San Francisco. My brain and body were numb. But where was Joe? I was to meet Joe Bowen here in Tokyo.

I boarded Northwest Flight #3. The plane didn't move. Finally, Joe and some other passengers entered the cabin. Their plane had been delayed in the U.S. We were happy to see one another.

We spent the night in Osaka. The next morning, July 2, 1974, we took off and made an intermediate stop in Okinawa. From the air Okinawa looked like an emerald surrounded by greenish-blue water and farther out the deep, rich blue of the Pacific.

Many memories came back. Okinawa had been a staging area for troops going to Vietnam, and that's where I had been headed six and a half years before.

Joe and I were on our way to a happier destination this time — Taipei, Taiwan — because my father had become intrigued with the idea that Taiwan, which had had such great success in the Little League World Series, might have some players who could help the Cincinnati Reds someday.

Consequently, he had gotten the ball rolling by contacting Dr. Creighton Hale, the President of Little League Baseball, who in turn contacted Senator K.C. Hsieh of the Republic of China.

The airplane followed a glacier of clouds to Taiwan. As we made our approach we could see antiaircraft guns encircling Taipei's airport. Taiwan was gripped by a siege mentality at this time, very much fearing an invasion by Red China. Taiwan was an armed camp; soldiers were posted everywhere.

After surviving a mad dash through immigration and customs, we were met by Jim Hart, my brother's longtime friend, and Buti Lee. Both were teachers at the Taipei American School.

When we stepped out of the air-conditioned airport, we stepped into a huge steam bath. Taipei was dripping with humidity. Buti drove us to our hotel.

Chinese drivers drove like kamikazes. It was so unsettling that I learned to buy a newspaper and never take my eyes off it when I rode in a taxi. Nothing in my experience — Rome, Paris, or Mexico City — could match the crazy driving habits of Taipei.

We ate lunch at Fung Lum restaurant. The food was delicious. I had minced pigeon, watermelon, and Taiwan beer. It was a real adventure every time you drank a brown bottle of Taiwan beer, since there was no government regulation controlling its alcoholic content. We dropped off Jim back at the hotel, and the three of us drove to the National Palace Museum where we viewed exquisite Chinese works of art, some dating back 4,000 years.

Afterwards, on a whim, we decided to bathe in hot sulfur water. The massage that followed was no massage; it was a physical beating by male attendants. I heard Joe at one point yell, "Knock off that crap!" My shoulders ached for two days.

I was a zombie after we ate dinner at an American-style restaurant. I watched a violent samurai movie on TV until I fell asleep.

The next morning Buti drove us to the Taipei City Baseball Stadium. We were scouting a tournament that had the best high school teams in Taiwan playing for nine straight days, three games a day. The ushers were fully armed soldiers. It was a new experience to have your ticket taken at a baseball game by an unsmiling soldier wearing a helmet, carrying an automatic rifle, and dressed in combat fatigues.

The infield was being dragged by a motorcycle as we sat in our seats. Coolie hats and black umbrellas dotted the crowd. Umpires wore blue pants, white shirts, and white gloves.

The Japanese influence on Taiwanese baseball was unmistakable. The team bowed to the fungo hitter before taking infield practice. The teams bowed to one another before the game started. Each hitter saluted and bowed to the home plate umpire before he stepped into the batter's box. A player who wanted to argue a call with an umpire first took off his hat, and then bowed after the argument was over. A pitcher who had hit a batter took off his hat and bowed to him.

The Japanese had introduced baseball to Taiwan — they had occupied Taiwan from 1895 to 1945 — but baseball didn't become the national rage until Taiwan won its first Little League World Series in 1969.

Watching the Chinese play baseball was like watching baseball being played in a different era. There were many ground balls as hitters tried to punch the ball through the infield. The idea wasn't to play for the big inning, but to play for one run. Teams didn't beat themselves by making errors; execution was nearly flawless.

If I were to compare the American player to the Chinese player, I would say in general that the American player is bigger, stronger, and swifter; the Chinese player is quicker, better trained, executes better, and is more disciplined.

There were differences between Chinese and American pitchers as well. Chinese pitchers tended to have pauses in their deliveries. In addition, Chinese pitchers pitched much more often — at least every other day.

With all the show of respect for authority, I was astounded to see a lengthy rhubarb on the first day of the tournament. An umpire and coach really got into it. Afterwards a tournament official explained the ruling to the crowd.

I talked to one of the few American spectators at the game, a serviceman, and he said the Chinese were too regimented, burned out too early, threw curveballs at too early an age, and had no fun playing the game. I hadn't been in Taiwan long enough to form strong opinions one way or the other, but I disagreed with one of his points. It seemed to me that the Chinese players were having fun playing the game.

Joe and I were engulfed by reporters at the tournament. They asked questions like: What is the purpose of your trip? Whom do you represent? How do you compare the Chinese teams with the American teams?

One reporter even offered to set us up with girls. Holy Cheongsam! Another reporter, Pao Yun-Min, an enterprising, persistent, and likable fellow, had Joe and me write articles for his Chinese newspaper. It was strange to see what I had written translated into Chinese characters.

I became good friends with Mr. Pao, and on subsequent trips he sometimes would take me around Taipei on his motor scooter.

We didn't see any prospects on the first two days of the tournament, but on the third day our luck changed. We saw two 18-year-old boys who impressed us: Kao Eng-Jey, a left-handed pitcher, and Lee Lai-Hua, a catcher.

Kao Eng-Jey was an intense competitor and a good athlete. He had a fine athletic physique (6-0, 175), a major league fastball, a fair curveball, and showed the makings of an effective change of pace. Temperamentally, he was somewhat of a moody individual. Had Kao been an American pitcher, he would have been a first round pick.

Lee Lai-Hua was the quickest and most agile catcher I have ever seen. He was 5-11, 170, had good hands, was a good runner, and had a decent bat. His big drawback was that he had only a marginal arm. But Lee played the game with joy. A signable boy.

During our ten-day stay in Taipei we conducted two tryout camps/instructional clinics. These were well received. Both Kao and Lee participated, and both excelled. The Chinese coaches and players were so very curious. Spectators were fascinated too, and they crowded around waiting to see, hear, and experience everything. Buti Lee acted as our interpreter.

Joe and I didn't see any other prospects in the tournament, so we turned our energies to setting up a procedure so that we could sign Kao and Lee to professional contracts.

Naturally, we went through Senator Hsieh, who directed us to various governmental agencies. We ran into bureaucratic walls everywhere, but the whole process was intriguing. I enjoyed playing Henry Kissinger. Buti, who spoke Mandarin, Taiwanese, Japanese, as well as English, was our indispensable interpreter/translator.

Hanging above everything — like a guillotine ready to fall — was the fluid political situation of Taiwan vis-a-vis the United States. President Nixon had made his famous visit to Communist China in 1972. Diplomatic relations between Taiwan and the U.S. were strained. The political climate could change literally overnight.

There were more mundane matters to confront as well:

(1) Mandatory military service of two or three years
    required at age 20.
(2) Must have a visa to leave Taiwan to play baseball and
    then return in the off-season.

When we left Taiwan we certainly hadn't had all of our questions answered, but we had established a presence there.

Buti Lee was signed to represent the Cincinnati Reds in Taiwan. Buti, along with his spunky, American-born wife, Mary, would perform yeoman service for the Reds over the next few years.

A month later, in August, Kao and Lee were in Ft. Lauderdale, Florida, as members of Taiwan's national team playing in a world tournament. Our scouts there liked their abilities, and so did other scouts at the tournament. They now were generating considerable interest.

I was sent to Taiwan to sign Kao and Lee in January 1975. Joe Bowen had sent me a detailed list of instructions. Some of the key points were:

(1) Sign both players or neither.
(2) Both players must pass a physical by an accredited doctor in
    Taiwan, and must pass our club physical upon arrival at spring
    training.

(3) If they signed, Buti Lee was to teach the players English. He also was to lessen the impact of culture shock in any way possible.

When I arrived at my hotel in Taipei there was a message waiting for me to call the office in Cincinnati. I talked with the club's lawyer about a clause that was going to be inserted into the contracts. It was the most expensive telephone conversation I've ever had — $180 — but it later saved the Reds thousands of dollars.

The added clause stated that the bonus payment had to be made in the United States in U.S. currency, and the player had to be physically present with the club or its affiliate to receive it.

We offered Kao $30,000 as a signing bonus, and Lee $5,000. Separate negotiations took place in my room at the Grand Hotel with Buti, myself, the players, and the players' parents. The negotiations were tough and lengthy. Innumerable questions were asked, but finally everything was resolved and the players and their parents signed the contracts.

The Cincinnati Reds received widespread publicity when they announced the signing of Kao and Lee.

This story could have had a fairy tale ending: the first Chinese players signed by an American professional team go on to fame and fortune in the big leagues, bringing great honor to their most revered homeland. But it just wasn't meant to be. We never could get the players out of Taiwan to the United States to play baseball. International politics threw a spitball that no one could hit.

On the surface, it was military obligations, school obligations, Personal Invitation Letters that didn't satisfy visa officials, translations of the contracts that didn't satisfy officials from the Departments of Education and Physical Education, clearances from the local police, etc.

But, in truth, it was the perceptions of powerful men living thousands of miles away from one another in a world full of sound and fury that doomed the endeavor.

I went back to Taiwan a few more times. Buti and Mary Lee did everything possible to try and get Kao and Lee out of Taiwan, but acute frustration was starting to creep into their letters.

Our scouting venture in Taiwan ceased when the United States ended diplomatic relations with Taiwan in 1978.

*   *   *

I awoke in the darkness. I fumbled for my watch. It was nearly four. I tried to go back to sleep, but my eyelids wouldn't stay shut. I lay in bed thinking for a few moments, then decided to read. I read several pages, not really concentrating, turned off the light, lay there feeling tired, restless, and increasingly irritated by the jet lag, and finally got up.

I walked across the room, pulled open the curtains, unlocked the door, and stepped out onto the balcony. The city's lights, glaring from the blackness like stage lights, blinded me for an instant. I looked around and was surprised to see a steady line of people moving up the road under the huge arch gate and along the side of the hotel. What could be going on at this ungodly hour? I thought a moment more. Yes, why not?

I dressed hurriedly, took the elevator down to the lobby, passed through the lobby where the receptionist — curled up on a chair — was snoring, woke up an embarrassed doorman as he opened the large entrance doors, and slipped out into the night.

A quarter moon and the stars faintly illuminated the way. Farther on past the hotel the procession followed a path that forked off to the right from the road. A cart filled with hot tea, milk, and oily sticks (breakfast cakes) sat off to one side of the path. People clustered around the cart, talking, eating, and drinking.

The stream of people snaked its way slowly up the mountain. Some men beat their backs with towels; some women fanned themselves. A few old people with canes wobbled upwards. The mountain became much steeper and the dirt path changed into concrete steps. The pungent odor of burning incense filled the air. Unseen roosters crowed loudly, and voices could be heard up and down the mountain. The line of people thinned as some stopped to catch their breath and others disappeared on side trails.

The trees and vegetation thickened and closed in. The jungle's umbrella sealed off the sky. Breathing became more difficult. Sweat ran down my chest like crawling insects and dripped off my elbows. The smells of the jungle hadn't changed though, that certain stifling mustiness, wetness, and rottenness. The memories roared back and with them old fears. My pace quickened.

The steps led up until a large path bisected them. Smaller steps continued straight ahead but I followed most of the people and took the pathway to the left. As I walked, the lights from Taipei flickered like fireflies through the trees.

The path sloped gently upwards for a short time and then downwards onto a finger of the mountain. Here the path widened into flat, open areas. Everywhere people were doing Tai Chi exercises, or laughing or gossiping or contemplating. Off to both sides, terraced, small, flat areas were cut out from the trees, some with huts having stools and tables. A couple sat drinking hot tea from a thermos in one of them. Down the mountain through the trees I could see parts of temples, some with glowing incense sticks.

A man, perhaps sixty, exercising vigorously, kept slapping his back with swinging arms as he danced forward and backwards. His body, slick with sweat, glistened in the bluish glare from an overhead electric light. An old woman stretched her obese torso. A man, facing east, stood on a rock covered with Chinese characters. Someone chanted. A white-haired old man blew a whistle and a group of old people began to exercise in a circle. Staccato yells of those doing their martial arts exercises punctured the air.

I sat down on a rock, faced west, and watched the lights from the buildings reflect off the Tamsui River. Although the yellowish sky was growing whiter, I could barely make out a small boat easing its way up the river in the mist. I heard the whistle and rolling wheels of a train off in the distance. Flocks of pigeons passed high overhead. For the first time I became conscious of things very near, the butterflies, the dragonflies, and the breeze that nudged the tree branches back and forth.

The first rays of the sun struck the tops of the trees as I started to exercise. I had worked up a good sweat by the time a man came up and said, "Hello."

I replied, "How are you?"

The man could only smile, not knowing any more English, and walked away. Soon others were greeting me with a "Hello." It felt good to be welcomed.

I sat down again on the rock, observing this Chinese ritual of the morning. Then I turned around so I could see the river, the city, and the mountains beyond. I thought for a long time. There was much to think about.

Even more people were coming up the mountain as I started down. They stared but I did not stare back. Shrilling cicadas serenaded the entire mountain. I came to the place where the jungle closed in. Mosquitos buzzed around my head as I felt the same fears as before. Shortly, the slope gentled as I caught sight of the golden roof of the hotel with its upswept eaves.

Back in my room I went out onto the balcony. There below on the Chungshan Bridge I watched the people, walking and riding bicycles, some wearing coolie hats; I watched the motor scooters, motorcycles, taxis, cars, trucks, and buses spew black exhaust as they moved across the bridge. The morning rush hour had begun.

The author standing between his father,
Bob Howsam, (left) and Sparky Anderson.
(EDWIN HOWSAM COLLECTION)

11

Viewpoint

Robert "Bob" Howsam, Sr.

Minor League Executive of the Year — 1951, Denver, Class A
Minor League Executive of the Year — 1956, Denver, Class AAA
Major League Executive of the Year — 1973, Cincinnati

In 1948 my grandfather, Lee Howsam, my uncle, Earl Howsam, and my father bought the ball club in Denver. Denver was part of the six-team Class A Western League. The Denver Bears played their games at Merchants Park. It was "a park to be remembered as a ramshackle, badly-planned brickyard with no grass in the outfield, but plenty of rocks," wrote Frank Haraway in an article titled "One Hundred Years of Denver Baseball History." What sticks in my memory of Merchants Park is a painful encounter I had with splinters there. I was 4 years old.

Incidentally, shortstop George Genovese was the crowd favorite that year. Later I got to know George well. He was already a scouting legend with the San Francisco Giants on the West Coast when I started scouting in Arizona.

Anyway, the family immediately set about to build a new ball park. They purchased a dump from the city of Denver at West 23rd Avenue and Clay Street for $32,000, and work began in earnest on Bears Stadium. The land and stadium were financed by selling bonds to individuals.

Bears Stadium opened on August 14, 1948 with 10,000 seats in place. Much later Bears Stadium would become Mile High Stadium —home of the Denver Broncos — and in 1993 and 1994 Mile High Stadium served as the temporary home of the Colorado Rockies, the new expansion team of the National League.

In 1949 Denver shocked the baseball world by drawing 463,039. This was nearly 200,000 more fans than the St. Louis Browns of the American League drew in 1949. Attendance averaged more than 400,000 during a five-year period, and for a ten-year period from 1949 to 1958, Denver outdrew every team in minor league baseball.

Of course, I wasn't greatly concerned about this as a boy. I just liked to go to the games and root for the Bears, chase foul balls, eat peanuts and Cracker Jacks, drink lemonade, and when the 7th inning stretch came, my mother would take her younger son — the one with such heavy eyelids — to the car so that he could get some shut-eye.

Because my father was running a minor league team, I became aware of the weather at an early age. In a sense, I was a farmer's son. What was the forecast for the day? Would it be sunny? Would it rain? Or — not unheard of in Denver — would it snow? Weather not only affects crops, but also the attendance at baseball games. I can remember my father searching the sky for answers, and sometimes I would hear the worry in his voice.

Some of the players I grew up watching were Tony Kubek, Bobby Richardson, Marv Throneberry, Ralph Terry, Whitey Herzog, Darrell Johnson and Don Larsen.

The manager I remember best from the early 1950s was Andy Cohen, who was extremely popular with the fans and players alike. Andy had once played second base for John McGraw with the New York Giants.

I ran into Andy again when I started scouting — he was the baseball coach at UTEP. At times Andy and his brother, Sid, who gave up Babe Ruth's last home run in the American League, would help at the tryout camp in El Paso. Both were gentlemen and colorful characters and Andy, who had been a vaudeville comedian, kept me in stitches all the time. In the summer when I scouted the El Paso Diablos of the Texas League, I always visited the Cohen family.

Over the years I had many different jobs with the Denver Bears. I pulled weeds on the hills outside the stadium, I helped on the scoreboard, I shined shoes with the clubhouse boy; I helped the groundskeeper by watering the field, mowing the grass on a tractor, painting home plate and the bases, setting up and removing the batting cage, laying down the foul lines and batter's box, wetting down the infield before the game, and raking the pitcher's mound and home plate. I also sold concessions, and for two years I was the bat boy of the Denver Bears.

1957 was a glorious year. It was my first year as the bat boy. I was in seventh grade. Ralph Houk was the manager and the Bears won the Junior World Series. I learned to spit, to curse, and many other useful things that year.

I remember playing pepper with Ed Donnelly, a left-handed pitcher, for Cokes. (Boot the ball and you owed the other guy a Coke.) Donnelly would become Denver's all-time leader in victories with 56. I also tried to catch towering pop-ups hit off Ben Flowers' fungo bat. Flowers, a big, right-handed pitcher, had the reputation of being able to hit the highest pop-ups in baseball. I would run around in circles but never touch the ball. Finally, Ben revealed the "secret." He taught me about the spin of the ball coming off the bat. After that, I started facing the right way and catching his pop-ups. Another big, right-handed pitcher, Marc Freeman, gave me a different type of education. This highly literate, intelligent gentleman from the South taught me a new word every night in the dugout. I remember the first word he ever taught me. The word was gullible.

Norm Siebern, an outfielder, was my favorite player on the team. Siebern just about led the American Association in every offensive category. Norm was big, quiet, friendly, and talented. He was my hero. I tried to wear my uniform the way he did, I tried to swing the bat the way he did, and I tried to act the way he did. I still have a photograph of me congratulating him at home plate after he had hit a home run. He wrote on the photograph, "Best Wishes to my buddy, Ed. Norm Siebern."

I can vividly remember when Ryne Duren joined the club a month into the season. He was down warming up in the bullpen and many of the players were watching him. The pop from the catcher's glove could be heard all over the stadium. Later he pitched the only Triple A no-hitter in Bears Stadium. He simply overpowered hitters; he threw fire.

Duren wore glasses that were as thick as Coke bottles. One of his favorite ploys when he was warming up before the game was to throw a ball halfway up the screen — that got the opposing team's attention in a hurry. And then he would take a big handkerchief out of his back pocket and start blowing on and rubbing those Coke bottles for a long time. After that, no one, and I mean no one, wanted to hit against him. Duren was scary.

Ralph Houk was one of the most likable men I've ever met. He had the rare trait as a manager to not only be respected by his players, but also to be liked. He was a gentleman but he also was one tough guy. Ralph loved to fight. He had been decorated in the war; in fact, his nickname was "Major."

The Bears started out of the blocks slowly in 1957, but they came on like gangbusters in the second half of the season. But at one point during the second half they went into a little slump. Houk wasn't happy, so he called a team meeting. A left-handed pitcher by the name of Tommy Lasorda had just joined the club and he was going to start the game. Lasorda was over the hill by then, but he still had a good curveball. Houk told the team that they needed a fight to rouse themselves out of the slump. Lasorda asked him in what inning he wanted the fight to start.

Denver was playing St. Paul. St. Paul had a first baseman with good power by the name of Norm Larker. Lasorda knocked Larker down with a high, hard one. They exchanged words and Larker charged the mound.

Lasorda, who had gotten the ball back from the catcher, wound up and just missed hitting the charging Larker in the face with the ball. They started fighting. Both dugouts emptied onto the field. Then I saw something that I have never seen since. Both teams formed a circle and wouldn't let the umpires break up a fight between Houk and St. Paul's manager, Max Macon. Houk beat the living hell out of Macon. I was told later by a Denver player that the St. Paul players so disliked their own manager that they had formed the circle first.

There's an amusing epilogue to this story. Years later in Albuquerque I ran into Tommy Lasorda, who was managing the Albuquerque club. Incidentally, that 1972 Albuquerque Dukes team was the best minor league team I've ever seen. They had players like Davey Lopes, Ron Cey, Tom Paciorek, Larry Hisle, Von Joshua, Joe Ferguson, Steve Yeager, Charlie Hough, Rick Rhoden, Doug Rau, Eddie Solomon, Jerry Stephenson, Stan Wall, Bruce Ellingsen, and Geoff Zahn. Hell, Paul Ray Powell was hitting eighth in the lineup, and he was hitting over .300.

Anyway, after the games, the two managers and some of the scouts would go over to Frank and Shirley Schifani's home to shoot pool, eat spaghetti, and talk baseball into the wee hours of the morning. One time I mentioned to Lasorda about his fight with Norm Larker. He told me that I hadn't heard the rest of the story.

It seems that years later Lasorda was back home in Pennsylvania eating at an Italian restaurant one wintry night, and in walked Norm Larker, who also was from Pennsylvania. They were both happy to see one another, and Larker sat down at Lasorda's table and started eating dinner with him. Naturally, they started talking baseball. Sooner or later the subject rolled around about the fight, and Larker kidded Lasorda about how he had beaten him up, and Lasorda said no, that he had beaten Larker up. They got into an argument, and things got so heated that they decided to go outside and settle it once and for all. They went outside and it was snowing. They looked at each other and decided that this was crazy, so they put their jackets back on, put their arms around one another, walked back into the restaurant, and finished the meal together.

*   *   *

One of the great rewards about becoming a scout with the Cincinnati Reds was that I was able to see my father in a new light. I saw how well he treated the scouts and other employees, and how highly respected he was by them. I could appreciate him not only as a father, but as "the boss" as well.

There are few people who can say they fulfilled their dreams in life. My father can. What he accomplished in his baseball career was amazing. He had a Hall of Fame career. He was the best GM of his era.

*   *   *

Interview — August 6, 1989

You spent a long apprenticeship in the minor leagues. What did the minor leagues teach you?

Well, the minor leagues was the start of learning baseball from the operational standpoint, and because there's so few people in the organization, you have to do a little of everything. For example, if there's a heavy rain, then sometimes the people in the front office have to go down and work on the field. You're greatly concerned about the cleanliness of the ballpark and parking lots. You have to know the costs of the concessions so that the fan isn't being overcharged, that the quality of the products is good, and once again that everything is clean.

You learn about crowd control. You learn how to treat people buying tickets, passing through the entrance gates, and being seated. Of course, the main attraction is your ball club on the field. I've always thought of the field as a stage, and this too must be attractive, and I've always considered the players to be performers in uniforms and these must be worn properly.

Ideally you want to have a well-qualified manager who's able to think ahead of the opposing manager so he'll win games by his strategy and knowledge. Players — if they don't hustle — won't get the fans to react to them. A hustling ball club that isn't winning as much as you'd like can overcome some of that, but make no mistake about it, winning is a very important part of the game.

The basic promotions are a winning team and a clean, well-run ballpark. Other promotions we used were always targeted for one group: company nights, town nights, farmers night, businessmen specials, ladies night, and so on. The one group we really went after was young people because they're the future of the game. We had promotions for youth teams, safety patrols, knothole gangs, straight A students, etc.

We weren't afraid to experiment in the minor leagues either. We tried different color bases and base lines, strike zone uniforms, which, incidentally, the umpires liked, and a gold baseball 20 years before Finley ever thought of the idea, but a gold baseball used on a dirt infield darkens too much at night and becomes dangerous.

You were the general manager of five teams that played in the World Series. Three of those teams were winners — St. Louis in 1964, and Cincinnati in 1975 and 1976. Which championship meant the most?

When you start out the first one seems to be so important to you, but there's no doubt it was the last one that meant the most to me because we swept the Phillies in three games in the championship series, and then we swept the Yankees in four games in the World Series. That had never been done before nor has it been done since.

What were some of the good trades that you made?

In St. Louis I had two of the finest trades I ever made, getting Orlando Cepeda from San Francisco and Roger Maris from New York. I needed a fourth place hitter and Cepeda became the National League MVP in 1967. Maris was a great influence on the club and solidified the team.

In Cincinnati I got Jim Merritt from Minnesota and he became a 20-game winner in 1970. Another favorable trade for Cincinnati was when I got Joe Morgan, Jack Billingham, Cesar Geronimo, Denis Menke and Ed Armbrister from Houston. Another big trade was getting George Foster from San Francisco, who later hit 52 home runs for us.

What were some of the bad trades that you made?

Well, a person is inclined to forget them, but the trade that was very harmful to the club was when I traded Tony Perez to Montreal. We lost a man who was very helpful in the clubhouse and who drove in a lot of big runs for us.

Did you have a basic philosophy for making trades?

Yes. I made trades for three reasons: (1) only to improve my ball club, (2) I tried to build a club to fit the stadium, and (3) I was always trying to upgrade the club with speed.

Are there some secrets in making good trades?

I don't know if there are any secrets, but it all starts with hard work. We spent many hours finding out everything we could about a player — on and off the field. Naturally, we were always analyzing our own team to discover our needs, and then we would analyze all the other teams in baseball to find out their needs. I got this information from scouting reports and by talking to the other general managers. Then we would break down the trades into priorities. We would try to have all this in place as the season ended.

Who were your mentors?

The first one I always think of is my father. He was tremendously interested in sports and had played sports. He was not only a great inspiration to me but also a great friend. Another person who had a lot to do with my life was my father-in-law, Senator Ed Johnson, who was one of the reasons I was able to get into professional baseball.

In professional baseball I became associated with Branch Rickey and George Weiss, who, at different times, provided players for teams in Denver. In my mind they were the two greatest minds in baseball, and the two greatest general managers in the history of the game. I tried to take the best from each and fit it into my approach.

I spent a number of years with Mr. Rickey watching him observe, test, and comment on talent, talk about baseball in general, talk about how to build a club, how to balance a club, and so on. He was a man of great ideas and was very much ahead of all the thinking in baseball.

The other one who had had such tremendous success was George Weiss. Unlike Branch Rickey, he hadn't been a player or manager, but he had worked his way up the system of the New York Yankees. He was a very shrewd man; he ran an extremely fine stadium; his judgment on his scouts was outstanding; and he was the best general manager at making deals going into the World Series in the history of the game.

One time I was visiting him at his home in Connecticut — he was showing me his baseball mementos — and I asked him how many diamond rings from World Series winners he had received during his years with the Yankees. He showed me 19 diamond rings. Nineteen!

Talk about Branch Rickey the man.

Branch Rickey was brilliant. He would have been successful in anything. He was a wonderful public speaker; he could mesmerize an audience like no one I've ever heard. He was spellbinding. He could bring an audience to its feet.

Mr. Rickey was a very religious man. He wouldn't go to games on Sunday because his mother had asked him not to. He didn't curse, of course, and the strongest words I ever heard him use were "Judas Priest." Mr. Rickey was tough at contract time because he had to be. He didn't have any money to work with. That's why he developed the farm system. I think he had 28 farm clubs at one time when he was with St. Louis. In some leagues he had more than one club.

Mr. Rickey also loved to fish. One time I was down in Cuba. The Pittsburgh Pirates were training in Havana, and we were going to have a working agreement with Pittsburgh that year. Mr. Rickey was so nice to me and one day he asked me if I would like to go fishing. So the next morning we met and here was Mrs. Rickey, and her sister, Annie, who couldn't have weighed ninety pounds soaking wet.

We drove all the way across Cuba to the place where we were going to fish. Mr. Rickey had lined up two guides and two row boats for us. Well, these two row boats were in such bad shape that you wouldn't have rowed them across the lake in City Park in Denver for fear they might sink, let alone take them out in the ocean. The oars were all wired together where they had been broken.

Anyway, the guides rowed the two boats out in the ocean. Someone caught a small shark but the fishing was slow. A commercial fishing boat came in not too far from us and started to sort fish. They were putting the larger fish into boxes and throwing the smaller ones into the ocean. Our guides rowed us to where they were throwing the smaller fish into the water, and for the next hour we had sensational fishing. We didn't even use bait. The water was just churning with tarpon. A person would throw in a silver hook about four or five inches long and he had a tarpon on. They would make these spectacular leaps and shake their heads. I was scared to death that one of those big tarpon that weighed as much as Annie might pull her out of the boat. We only landed three tarpon, but that was an unforgettable fishing trip.

And Mr. Rickey was an unforgettable man.

You talked about George Weiss of the Yankees. What type of guy was Casey Stengel?

Undoubtedly, Casey Stengel was one of the great characters in baseball history. I'll give you a quick story. Casey and Del Webb, the part owner of the Yankees, flew into Denver in the winter of 1955 because we were moving up from Class A to Triple A, and we had a new working agreement with the Yankees. I met Frank Haraway, the baseball writer for *The Denver Post*, at the airport. I told Frank that he should take Mr. Webb, because his dad had been a friend of Mr. Webb, and I'd take Casey. We were going to have breakfast at the Denver Country Club, and then we were going to a press conference downtown which was scheduled for 10:00 a.m.

Anyway, the Yankees had just made a deal with the Baltimore Orioles, and I asked Casey what he thought about the deal. He told me in great detail everything about every player in the deal. He evaluated the deal from every standpoint. It was a perfect report.

So we ate breakfast and went down to the press conference. Someone asked Casey a question, and he started talking Stengelese and nobody knew what he was saying.

But when he wanted to be, he was a very sharp fellow.

As the architect of the Big Red Machine, how did you go about creating it?

There was a foundation when I first went to Cincinnati in 1967 with Tony Perez, Pete Rose, and Gary Nolan. We brought Bench up from the farm system the next year. In 1970 I hired Sparky Anderson to manage the club. Concepcion and Gullet came up. We traded for Foster in 1971. We made the big trade with Houston in 1972 for Morgan, Billingham, Geronimo, and the others. Driessen came up the following year. Griffey in 1974. Now all the parts of the Big Red Machine were in place.

So it was a matter of utilizing several players already at Cincinnati, developing others through the farm system, making sound trades, and hiring the right manager.

Let's play a word association game. I'll give you a name and you respond with a word or a short comment.

Sparky Anderson — knew how to use his players, a hard worker, a winner.
Johnny Bench — the greatest catcher in the history of the game.
Tony Perez — a tremendous RBI man and a tremendous asset to a ball club.
Joe Morgan — the best offensive player I've ever seen.
Davey Concepcion — the finest all-around shortstop I've seen in baseball.
Pete Rose — a tremendous hustler and a great hitter.
Danny Driessen — a good, steady ballplayer.
George Foster — great power.
Cesar Geronimo — one of the best defensive center fielders I ever saw.
Ken Griffey — an outstanding all-around ballplayer.
Jack Billingham — a clutch pitcher.
Don Gullett — one of the better left-handers of his era.
Fred Norman — knew how to pitch and win.
Gary Nolan — one of the best young pitchers I've seen come into the game.
Pedro Borbon — a real character, a great competitor, had a rubber arm.
Clay Carroll — one of the best relief pitchers I ever saw, he *wanted* the ball.
Will McEnaney — a fine relief pitcher.

Rawly Eastwick — like McEnaney, a fine relief pitcher, but right-handed.

Many experts consider the 1976 Cincinnati Reds to be one of the top three teams in baseball history. Yet essentially the same team finished 10 games back of the Dodgers in 1977. Why?

I felt we should have won, but complacency was a problem, plus I had traded Tony Perez to Montreal.

Why did Marvin Miller, who represented the players, have such incredible success against the owners?

Basically because the union has leverage. Marvin Miller was intelligent, hard working, knew his stuff, and took advantage of a group of mostly inexperienced owners who were overly anxious to compromise.

What has free agency meant to the game?

It means that salaries can run rampant. And I don't like the six-year rule because you can lose your good ballplayers right in their prime. With guaranteed contracts, some players don't play as hard as they should because they get paid whether they play or not.

Is it possible for a general manager to build a great team in this day and age?

I think it is. You see some very good teams today. Maybe you can't balance them as well today, but if you'll use the basic programs — good scouting, a good minor league developmental program, a good manager and coaching staff, and continue to work hard to improve your players even at the major league level — then I think you can still build good teams.

What has arbitration done to the salary structure?

Arbitration is one of the worst things that we in baseball ever accepted, and the reason for this is before you ever go to arbitration, ball clubs offer the players more money than they normally would just to keep the players out of arbitration. Plus you have arbitrators who have no background in why you would or would not give a player a raise. This has caused some players who have only had one good year to receive salaries that are completely out of line.

The arbitration process itself is a very negative experience. It creates hard feelings. Who really wins? It can be an embittering experience for both parties, no matter who wins because no player likes to have his performance torn apart, and no organization likes to give away money.

Will we see the day of the twenty-million-dollar-a-year ballplayer?

I don't know, but the way fans are supporting baseball now and the way TV contracts are, it's not out of the realm of possibility. We might see astronomical salaries someday if pay-per-view ever catches on. On the other hand, you might see salary reductions if there is a low period in the economy which in turn causes lack of fan support.

What is your opinion of ownership?

Ownership itself has caused as many problems as the union. Some owners don't seem to realize that because they're in a league, whatever they do causes others to follow along thinking that this is the only way they can remain competitive. This is the domino effect in practice, especially with salaries.

It's a black mark on baseball that the scouts, minor league managers and instructors, and front office people aren't paid a better, more proportionate share of what baseball makes.

Do the agents control today's game?

Another certainty in life — besides death and taxes — is when there is big money around, there are agents around. They're playing with a strong hand. After all, an agent might be the deciding factor if a player signs or re-signs with your club. Also, there's plenty of potential for abuse, not only against the clubs but against the players themselves.

Is baseball fun anymore for the general manager?

I hope so. But I can remember before I left the game, when general managers would get together and talk about how the game had changed, and over and over it was said that it wasn't fun anymore.

In your 40-plus year association with professional baseball, how has the game changed on the field?

For one thing, the umpires have become more belligerent. As far as the players, there are many more injuries today than there ever was before. I think there are better athletes playing the game today, but in most cases I don't see the same effort on the field that I used to see. Many players are rushed to the major leagues; consequently, they haven't learned the finer points of the game. Overall, I don't think the game today is played as well as it was.

I have never liked the DH. It takes away much of what the game is all about, the excitement of making moves at the end of the game. Every fan is a manager in the stands, and the DH doesn't allow him to participate in the strategy of the game.

Of course, we have seen the specialization of pitching. This has changed the game. You can't win without good relief pitching.

How morally healthy is the game today?

I'm afraid we have hit a low point caused by drugs, alcohol, gambling, values. I hope we can lift it back up to where it belongs. We must if we want to keep the trust of the American people.

You not only put together some great teams on the field in Cincinnati, but you also built a great organization. How did you do this?

I'm a believer that the signing of young ballplayers and the developing of young ballplayers is of the upmost importance; therefore, I tried to get together the finest group of scouts and minor league managers and instructors that I could.

Moreover, I believe that an organization is like a team. People don't work for you; we work together. It's vital to have *esprit de corps* because people work harder, they're truly interested in what happens, and they're proud to be part of it.

I also believe in paying decent wages, having good benefits such as a profit-sharing program, a pension plan, medical and dental insurance, and we even paid out bonuses to all our people when the team did well. The idea is to retain good people and to pull together as a team.

What is the importance of scouting?

Scouting is the lifeblood of your organization. It's the starting point for building your team.

Were your scouts given special instructions?

Just to work hard, cover their territory completely by going to remote places, small towns, small colleges, inner city playgrounds; be persistent, don't be put off by the weather, see players more than once if possible, and don't make judgments too quickly.

What is your opinion of the Major League Scouting Bureau?

I don't like it because I want my own scouting staff.

What was your biggest thrill in baseball?

That's hard to say. But really the biggest thrill for me in baseball was when I walked out into that stadium during a game and I saw so many people of all ages, all backgrounds, all nationalities, and all colors enjoying the game of baseball.

Do you have any regrets in your baseball career?

I'm terribly saddened by the Pete Rose affair.

What about Pete? Talk about Rose the player.

Pete made more of his talents than any player I've ever seen. He gave everything he had. There's no doubt he was a great hitter. He had a great eye at the plate, great reflexes, and quick hands. But he also created the illusion that he could do more on the field than he really could, and that's to his credit. The opposition bought it. For example, he wasn't a fast runner but he gave you the impression he was. He would hustle down to first base after getting a base hit and knock his cap off in the process. That gave everyone the impression that he could run. He would do the same thing while chasing a ball in the outfield, and it looked like he was running out from underneath his cap. This too gave the illusion of speed. Do you realize that he didn't steal *one* base in 162 games in 1975, the year we won the World Series against Boston?

Rose was a very smart player because he understood his limitations and capabilities better than anyone else. After all, he was the first player to be paid $100,000 without having home run power.

What about Rose the person?

Unfortunately, Rose didn't measure up as a good husband or good father in my observations.

When did you first learn about his gambling habits?

Everyone in Cincinnati seemed to know that he bet the horses heavily. But that was legal. I heard after he left Cincinnati that he wasn't paying off his gambling debts, and "they" were going to get him after he stopped playing.

Did you know that he had a serious addiction to gambling?

No. I never had an idea that he was doing what he did. If I had known, I would never have brought him back to Cincinnati. I was shocked when everything came out. I thought Rose was going to be an outstanding manager.

Why didn't he become an outstanding manager?

He wouldn't listen to anybody. And if you're not going to listen to people, then how are you going to learn, to develop, and to grow into a difficult job? Just because you're a great player doesn't mean you're going to be a great manager. Pete could motivate and even inspire his teammates when he was playing with his hustling style of play, but when he was the manager — not playing and sitting in the dugout — he didn't have the same effect on the team.

Does Pete Rose belong in the Hall of Fame?

Definitely not, if he bet on baseball and the Reds. And I don't think Reuven Katz — Rose's attorney and agent, and a very sharp fellow — would have made the deal he did with baseball unless Rose had bet on baseball and the Reds.

What will baseball be like in 100 years?

There is an old saying in baseball that baseball succeeds in spite of itself. I hope in 100 years everyone in the game is giving his best effort to keep baseball the great American game.

How do you want to be remembered?

I guess I want to be remembered as just one of the boys of baseball.

NOTABLE QUOTES

"More than anything he loved the game, and when you love the game of baseball you eat it and sleep it and are bound to succeed if you got the stuff to go with it."

— Mark Harris
The Southpaw

"Yeah, Howsam, I know why you went to Taiwan. Not to scout, but to tie one on."

— Dick McLaughlin
Minor League Instructor,
Los Angeles Dodgers

The immortal Lou Gehrig and Babe Ruth.
(EDWIN HOWSAM COLLECTION)

12

Graffiti

Baseball is an ethereal game whose music is orchestrated by a moving sphere.

Baseball's fulcrum is home plate. The action begins there, and ultimately the game is won or lost there. Great, small, and non-collisions occur there with regularity. Bat meets ball; bat doesn't meet ball. The non-struck ball can be a thing of beauty, but the struck ball powers the game into motion. Baseball's excitement is derived from that released energy.

*   *   *

Scouting

Artists and baseball scouts have one thing in common, they both try to *see*, not just look.

The scout's job is to discover and contract good baseball players. A psychologist might put it differently, i.e., the scout's purpose is to explain and predict human behavior based on previous experience.

Where does a scout sit at a game? If he's using a radar gun, he *must* sit behind home plate. (Radar guns can measure the speed of a ball accurately only when it's traveling in a straight line.) Other reasons why a scout might choose to sit behind home plate are to see the movement and location of every pitch, the pitcher's delivery, the catcher's throwing accuracy, footwork, and how he calls a game, and the strengths and weaknesses of a hitter.

A scout sits off to the side to see a pitcher's arm action, leg action, pick-off move to first base, the catcher's hands, the hitter's hands, stance, and bat speed, to get a different perspective of the infielders and outfielders, and to have a better angle to time runners running from home plate to first base with a stopwatch.

He sits in the upper deck because he has a wonderful view for evaluating infield and outfield play. If a scout is sitting in the bleachers, sunning his bod, checking out the lovelies, drinking a cold one — he'll soon be an ex-scout

Ultimately, scouting comes down to comparisons. The scout is incessantly comparing what he sees on the high school, college, and minor league diamonds to the big leagues.

Baseball is a form of entertainment, as is listening to the Philadelphia Symphony, or watching a Steven Spielberg film. A baseball scout goes to a game to be entertained by individuals. Someone must do something that catches his eye, or attracts his attention, or if you will, entertains him. It's a different facet of the game because the scout doesn't care what the score is, or who is winning or losing the game. He's focusing narrowly on individual performances.

The ideal everyday ballplayer is the one who has the five pluses: run, throw, field, hit, and hit with power.

The Moon is 238,000 miles from Earth. If you take the number of miles that I drove for the Reds in 17 years, I could have driven to and from the Moon. That's a lot of lonely miles on the highway.

One time I stepped into a time warp when I was scouting a player in Deming, New Mexico. I had to pinch myself to see if I were dreaming. I wasn't. Cars and pickups were lined up along both foul lines, and depending on which team scored or made a good play, the cars and trucks along one foul line would honk their horns.

Baseball radar guns differ in their readings because they are designed for different purposes. Scouts use two different types of radar guns: the Jugs and the Ra-Gun.

The Jugs gets a faster reading because it's designed to pick up the pitched ball somewhere between 3 to 5 feet after it leaves the pitcher's hand. Jugs believes this early reading eliminates variables, thus ensuring consistency.

The Ra-Gun gets a slower reading because it's designed to pick up the pitched ball near home plate (after the ball has lost some of its speed). Ra-Gun believes this later reading is the most important because this is where the issue is settled, at home plate.

An average major league fastball on the Jugs is 90 mph; on the Ra-Gun it's 86 mph.

It's extremely difficult to find good catchers. If I were designing a player to play in the big leagues quickly, it would be a left-handed hitting catcher who could throw, catch, call an intelligent game, and take charge.

Once I had a dream that I was driving down a dusty road in the middle of nowhere, and I saw this Mexican kid throwing a rock at a cactus. I slammed on the brakes. He threw another rock. He had a perfect delivery and he had thrown the rock over 100 mph. I went over to talk to him but he couldn't speak English. I ended up signing him, and he ended up winning 300 games in the big leagues. I woke up just as he was being inducted into the Hall of Fame.

*   *   *

The Draft

The baseball draft is pure socialism. The draft's intent is to create competitive balance. It's a response to the question: What is best for baseball?

How to position yourself to be drafted: persist, be seen, seek good competition and instruction, play in a good college program, attend a good baseball school, play for a good summer team, attend tryout camps.

A baseball scout wears two hats. He's not only a judge of talent, but a negotiator as well. Complications arise any time you're dealing with money, but they're further complicated when you're dealing with inflated egos. Naturally, every parent thinks his boy is going to be the next Greg Maddux or Ken Griffey, Jr. Ever fascinating, sometimes frustrating, negotiations can be one of the most rewarding parts of scouting. There are few joys greater in life than to help someone else's dream come true.

In 1972 the Reds drafted Bob Cummings in the eight round from West

High School in Phoenix. He had an appointment to the Naval Academy as well as a baseball scholarship to the University of Arizona. I made the offer. The family decided to vote on the matter. The father, older brother, and Bob all voted to sign. The mother voted no.

I went out and bought a bottle of champagne, and we celebrated after Bob signed the contract.

The toughest father I ever negotiated with was Richard Mutz. Richard is a rancher in New Mexico, and the father of Tommy Mutz, the first player I ever signed. Tommy was a good-looking catcher from Cochise Junior College. The signing was very much in doubt until the mother made one of the most eloquent, beautiful, and touching statements I've ever heard. It was a scene out of the movies.

Fifteen years after I signed Tommy, I branded calves with Richard in Moriarty, New Mexico.

The Cincinnati Reds required every scout to give an eye test to any player who was going to be on his draft list. Each scout carried an eye tester, and it only took a few minutes to administer the test. The test was designed to pick out gross deficiencies. Rarely did a player have a problem with the test. If one did, he was sent to an ophthalmologist to have his eyes checked. Poor vision and depth perception problems are not pluses for a ballplayer.

I would advise parents of drafted players to let their son make the final decision. Obviously, it's a momentous decision. Families should discuss every consequence of signing or not signing. But I still believe that the young man should make the final decision.

It has been my experience that if a young man makes an important decision — no matter how it turns out — then he can live with it. But when someone else makes an important decision for him — and things don't work out — bitterness can linger for years.

Fathers play a significant role in the development of their sons. In baseball, as well as in life, this can be a positive or negative influence.

Over the years I have witnessed some disgusting behavior by a few fathers who were trying to live their dreams through their sons. They became possessed by the notion that their sons were going to play in the major leagues. They pressured, berated and punished their sons to obtain that goal.

Come on, dads, lighten up and keep it all in perspective. The chances of your son becoming a major leaguer are infinitely small. Fewer than 10% of the players who sign professional contracts ever make it to the big leagues.

With those odds stacked against your son, the goal of every father should be to make baseball as much fun as possible for the boy. If your son has the talent and desire to become a big league ballplayer, terrific — it's an American dream come true — but if not, don't make his memories of playing baseball wretched. Life's too short for such nonsense.

My advice to all fathers is to make time to attend your son's games. (If you don't, you'll be shocked at how fast he grows up.) Being there is vital. Cheer for him, of course, but cheer for the team as well. Stand by him, win or lose. Let him be a boy. This is a game, not a life or death situation. We're talking about a *lifetime* relationship here.

I used to watch Barry Bonds play at Arizona State. Whenever his father, Bobby Bonds, came to town I knew Barry would go into a slump. He always had his head in the stands looking for his dad while he was playing. Barry Bonds, a terrific college hitter, couldn't have hit *me* when his father was in town watching him play.

In 1990 I was watching the championship series between Cincinnati and Pittsburgh. Barry Bonds was struggling at the plate. Someone interviewed Bobby Bonds and asked him why his son wasn't hitting. Bobby went into a lengthy, detailed technical analysis on what Barry was doing wrong. I thought to myself, that's not the problem, Bobby, *you're* the problem.

*   *   *

Hitting & Pitching

I agree with Ted Williams' contention that the most difficult thing to do in sports is to hit successfully at the major league level. (Just ask Michael Jordan about hitting a baseball at the *minor* league level.) Think about it. Hitting a round ball traveling at nearly 100 mph with a round bat, and hitting it squarely.

The hitter has less than one second to make his decision. He has 2/5 of a second to decide where the ball is going, and when it will get there. If he decides the ball will be in the strike zone and he wants to swing, then he must make his response in 2/5 of a second.

Some variables that affect hitting are eye-hand coordination, reflexes, information processing, fear, intimidation, pressure, environmental elements, and the variety of pitches that can be thrown at different speeds.

No wonder if a hitter fails seven times and succeeds just three times, he's considered to be a good hitter.

Pitching is the disruption of the hitter's rhythm by the pitcher's rhythm.

The ideal pitcher is the one who possesses a great, live arm and who can, in any given situation, put any of his pitches wherever he chooses.

How do old pitchers stay in the big leagues when their fastballs are just memories? They're savvy and they can throw their breaking pitches for a strike.

Unless there has been an injury, usually the first thing to go on a pitcher is his legs, not his arm.

Arguably the most important player on a *contending* club doesn't even start the game. He's the closer — the short relief pitcher who "closes the door" on the other team at the end of a game.

You have just taken your seat at a big league stadium. Someone (hopefully not Roseanne Barr) has just sung the National Anthem. But don't buy a hot dog and beer yet. Concentrate on both pitchers in the early innings. If they aren't able to throw their breaking pitches — curveball, slider, etc. — for a strike, then there's a good chance they'll be taking early showers.

Even a great power pitcher like Nolan Ryan needed to establish his breaking pitch early in the game. Sure, he was able to get by with his blazing fastball, but if his curveball was working, then he had a chance to throw a no-hitter.

I saw Nolan throw a one-hitter against the San Diego Padres when he was 37 years old. He threw a few fastballs at 97 mph on my Jugs radar gun, but he had a very sharp breaking curveball working that day, and he had a great hitter like Tony Gwynn swinging at his curveball in the dirt.

I admire Sandy Koufax, the Hall of Famer, as a human being. I would watch him instruct young pitchers with the Dodgers Instructional League team in the fall. He never told them how to pitch, he only made suggestions.

I have seen many tough competitors in baseball, but I have never seen a tougher competitor than Gaylord Perry. I remember one spring training game Perry was pitching, and someone made an error in the outfield. Perry turned around on the mound and glared at the player for what seemed like a lifetime.

The word awesome has become a cliché in sports. However, J.R. Richards' performance against the Reds during the glory years of the Big Red Machine *was* awesome. I was back in Cincinnati for scouting meetings one September and Cincinnati was playing Houston, and Richards was on the mound for the Astros. Richards was intimidating because he stood 6-8, he was wild enough to keep the hitters honest, he could throw his fastball 100 mph, *and* he could throw his slider 93 mph. For six innings the Reds hardly hit a foul ball off Richards. He dominated one of the great hitting teams in the history of the game. Finally, he got wild, too wild, and the Reds got to him. But you don't forget performances like that.

*   *   *

Last At-Bat

The best all-around player I ever saw was Joe Morgan, 2B, Cincinnati Reds. He could beat you more ways than anyone else.

In any sport where speed plays an important part, it's by far the most decisive factor over a period of time.

What do I think about Pete Rose? A quotation from F. Scott Fitzgerald sums up my feelings: "Show me a hero and I will write you a tragedy."

Of the thousands of players I have scouted, the player who I think would make the best big league manager is Marty Barrett, an infielder who played with Boston and San Diego.

Barrett has two characteristics that aren't usually found in a baseball manager: superior intelligence and stonewall toughness.

In El Paso at the minor league games, they pass the hat after a home team player hits a home run. I haven't seen this done anywhere else. I love it.

I have ambivalent feelings about Little League. I've seen games that were fun for the youngsters, but I've also seen games that turned into adult horror shows: parents yelling at parents, parents yelling at coaches, parents yelling at players, coaches yelling at players, and coaches yelling at one another.

I was scouting a Pacific Coast League game in Las Vegas in the summer of 1984, and I was sitting behind home plate using my radar gun. A man sitting behind me started asking questions and we struck up a conversation.

He was very knowledgeable about baseball. He introduced himself and said his name was Dennis Gilbert. He said he was an agent, and he was watching some of his players and scouting other players in the league.

Dennis and I ran into each other later that summer in El Paso. We sat together and talked baseball. I was curious about what it was like to be an agent. He had played minor league baseball and had a background in insurance. I enjoyed talking with this agent whom I had never heard of.

I ran into Dennis a few times after that in minor league parks. Later I was shocked when I read in the newspaper during the winter of 1991-92 that Dennis had negotiated $54.5 million worth of contracts for just two players — Bobby Bonilla ($29 million) and Danny Tartabull ($25.5 million). This "small potatoes" agent had become the top agent in baseball.

Who is the nicest man in baseball? The envelope please . . . . . and the winner is Sparky Anderson. Sparky is a sure-fire Hall of Famer because he's the only manager in baseball history to have won the World Series in *both* leagues. He did it in the National League with the Cincinnati Reds in 1975 and 1976, and in the American League with the Detroit Tigers in 1984.

I've never met a man in baseball who has had such success and who is so modest, humble, and down-to-earth.

One man *can* make a difference. Ralph Meder did in Las Vegas. I met many people in 17 years of scouting, but none had as much influence on young men as Ralph.

Almost every Sunday during the off-season you could find Ralph working with young players. Scores of boys received college scholarships because of him, and he was instrumental in getting scouts to look at certain players. Players such as Mike Morgan, Marty and Tommy Barrett, Mike and Greg Maddux, and Danny Opperman owe much of their development to Ralph. Just ask them.

Ralph died a few years back, but he hasn't been forgotten. The city of Las Vegas named a field in his honor. No one was ever more deserving. A man doesn't have to be famous to be a great man.

The most amazing performance by a young athlete that I have ever seen occurred in the spring of 1974 when Robin Yount, 18 years old, made the Milwaukee Brewers club as a shortstop. Everything he did that spring was nearly perfect.

The Oakland A's, who won the World Series in 1972, 1973, and 1974, had a team composed of diverse characters, symbolized by Rollie Fingers' splendid mustache. Oakland had great team chemistry on the field, but off the field the players didn't mind throwing a few punches at one another.

Oakland's spring training games could be bizarre. Sometimes Catfish Hunter would lob the ball up to home plate and the other team would score 10 or 15 runs off him. Reggie Jackson, always the showman, would miss balls on purpose just to get a reaction from the fans. Yep, the Oakland A's were never boring.

CUBS MAGIC NUMBER: 9-1-1. This is the funniest banner I've ever seen. I saw it on TV at Wrigley Field when the Cubs were struggling in July 1990.

I detest the Designated Hitter (DH) rule. One time I was scouting in Australia when I heard one of the players ask the coach who was going to be the "Dick-Head" (DH) for the game. It's the appropriate expression.

I am fascinated by the Japanese approach to baseball. Take infield practice. Have you ever seen a fungo hitter hit pop-ups not only to the catcher but to all the infielders? And line drives as well?

One August evening I was in Tucson scouting a Pacific Coast League game. Pam Postema was umpiring behind home plate. Unfortunately, she wasn't having a good game calling balls and strikes. The Tucson bench started to ride her hard. Finally, she couldn't take it any longer and she jerked off her mask and strode angrily towards the Tucson dugout yelling, "Get off me! Get off me!" A loud voice boomed from the dugout, "Who in the hell would want to get on you?" She spun around in mid-stride and walked back to home plate.

College students can be like, well, college students. One time I was watching Wichita State play Arizona State in Tempe, Arizona. The Wichita State pitcher attempted to pick a runner off first base. One student brought the house down when he yelled, "Your mother's got a better move with a man on than you do!"

One of my favorite people in baseball is Eddie Cohen. Eddie is a beer vendor. Over the years we have become friends. I always stop to chat with him at the game. Eddie is the world's biggest San Francisco Giants fan. This has led to some lively exchanges. He never gives up on them. If the Giants were 20 games out of first place with 21 games to go in the season, Eddie would believe they could still win the pennant.

It was interesting to watch a spring training game in Sun City, Arizona. Senior citizens love their baseball, so attendance was good. Golf carts would line up at the top of the stadium down the first base line.

One time two senior citizens got into a shouting match, and much to the disbelief of all, it looked like punches were going to be thrown. Some old guy, sitting a couple of rows back of the antagonists, stood up and said in a loud voice, "Welcome, ladies and gentlemen, to the heavyweight championship fight of the world in s-l-o-o-o-o-o-w motion."

On September 14, 1994, a day of infamy in baseball history, the owners ended the baseball season. For the first time since 1904 there would be no World Series. Greed had felled baseball.

It appears that a far-reaching economic shakeout is underway as millionaire owners battle millionaire players for ever-increasing amounts of money. Where this will eventually take the game is anyone's guess. Baseball will be played again, but it will never be quite the same.

Unfortunately, throughout their skirmishes the players and owners have lost sight of one salient fact. Players come and go; owners come and go; but the millions of fans who have a love affair with baseball remain the one constant in the game. Should that love affair ever come to an end, baseball will be finished. Maybe that end hasn't been reached, but we can certainly see it from where we stand.

Last wish: When the last rays of light have faded, when the stadium gates have been locked, when the score is only a memory, my hope is that wherever I am, I'll be able to turn on the radio and listen to Vin Scully describe some distant game with his poetry.

NOTABLE QUOTES

*"Pitchers are like snowflakes — every
one of them is different."*

—Larry Doughty
Scouting Director, Cincinnati Reds

*"Yeah, Ed, I check the obituary
column every morning at breakfast, and
if I don't read my name in there,
I go scout a game."*

—Don Lindeberg
Scout, New York Yankees

Order Form

If you have enjoyed reading *Baseball Graffiti* and would like to order an additional copy (or copies), please complete the order blank.

Money back guarantee: I understand that I may return any book(s) for a full refund — for any reason, no questions asked.

Name:_____

Address:_____

City:_____

State:_____Zip:_____

Daytime Phone: (   )_____

Number of copies:_____ @ $12 each, plus $2.95 each for postage and handling. Total cost for each book: $14.95.

Please send Check or Money Order along with Order Form to:

EH Productions
8745 Via De La Luna
Scottsdale, Arizona 85258